I0711821

Who am I?

Self-knowledge and personal growth

ROSA DOMINGO

DEDICATION

My mother Antonia. Thank you for being
there whenever I've needed you.
With your light you have guided my way.

PROLOGUE

In Greek mythology there was a great master named Chiron. He was a centaur, that is, half man and half horse, and while centaurs were considered rough and wild beings, Chiron represented an exception among his own, since he was kind and very wise: he was a music teacher, an art and hunting enthusiast, a defender of morality, a medicine and surgery scholar, and time also made him tutor of great heroes of the Greek mythology such as Achilles or Jason, whom he trained in the use of weapons and other strategies of the warrior arts.

The figure of the centaur represents the dispute between civilization and barbarism because of its double half human and half animal condition. Somehow, when people ask questions to themselves we are fighting against our ignorance, in a desire to inwardly learn and develop. And that's where the teacher plays an important role, not only because of their ability to clearly convey knowledge but, above all, because they have lived that process in themselves.

In Japanese master is called «sensei» which means «the one who was born before». The only difference between the student and the teacher is considered to be that the teacher was born before and that is why they can teach the student something. In this way, we can always learn something from who is older than us. Therefore, they have the experience that one's life gives them.

On the other hand, the term used in Sanskrit to call a teacher is «guru»: «gu» means darkness and «ru» means light; so, the word guru means «the one who dissolves darkness». There is no doubt that learning is necessary for human development, and that human beings have an innate impulse toward knowledge and light.

There is also another aspect that, in my opinion, makes the teacher essential: his ability to transmit values. Values build us as people and are responsible for our way of being in the world, they bring us security, strength and trust. They represent a compass that guides us towards vital goals, and ultimately, give us the meaning of life.

This mentor figure was always attractive to me, and at an early age I dreamed of having a teacher to ask them the eternal questions and to guide me in life. However, that teacher as I had imagined never came, and instead of them, teachings were coming to me through other ways and in small pieces: my parents and brothers, a conference, a university professor, a personal growth course, a book, the internet... Then, I learned that a teacher can have many forms, and that we simply have to be prepared to warn his presence. As the Zen proverb says: «*A teacher arrives when the student is ready*».

For all those who have at some point shared the desire to have a teacher, here I leave you a little piece of the teacher that I have been building myself.

WHO AM I?

CONTENT

1
TO BE

One early morning of fall, Sophie went out the porch and saw her mother so focused on her laptop that she barely noticed her daughter was talking to her.

—Mom, what are you writing? —asked Sophie.

—I'm sorting out some ideas of courses I've done in the last years, I've got so many notes that I never find what I need—, replied her mother without raising her sight of the keyboard.

—What are these courses about? —said Sophie, getting close to her.

—These are «personal growth» courses. They are useful for learning important things in life and when you learn these things… you grow inside, — replied her mother with a smile. She was glad her daughter was curious.

—Mom! I didn't know adults were in the age to grow up! If you were, you'd have to go to school! —exclaimed Sophie cheerfully.

—I know Sophie, it is not obligatory for adults to go to school, but that doesn't mean that we know everything, there is still a lot to learn but life is complicated, especially if you have a partner, children, a job...; it is said that life teaches you, that it is already a school itself, but the truth is that a little help from time to time is not bad thing.

Sophie looked at the computer screen, and with a strange face, said:

—Why do you write in English?

—I don't write in English; I write a quote to start each topic. I love quotes! Look, —she said, pointing at the screen. I put it in italics and it looks super nice.

«To be or not to be, that is the question»
WILLIAM SHAKESPEARE

—What does it mean? —asked the girl.

—«To be or not be, that is the question» is the first verse of the third act of one of Shakespeare's most important plays, which is titled «Hamlet», is one of the most famous phrases in universal literature. Do you know it?

—It rings a bell... Why does he say that? Can you choose not to be? —asked Sophie, frowning.

—Well, yes, Sophie, you can choose not to be, but it's a long story, —said her mother.

—Can you explain it to me, mom? Sophie begged.

—Of course I can, daughter —said her mother—. This phrase is said by a young man named Hamlet, who considers a big decision about having to

avenge his murdered father or not; I use this quote to explain the dilemma of life between being yourself or being what others expect from us. Normally we talk about being when we describe ourselves. We say «I am» and then a series of data appear: I am white, I am a mother, I am a psychologist, I am cheerful, I am a writer, etc. We use being as our own identity. Being able to say «I am» means that we are aware of ourselves, but that consciousness seems a little shallow; that is, after the «I am» there is data that we could find in our ID or in the library card. To describe ourselves, we use adjectives about our appearance, our origin, our way of behaving with others...

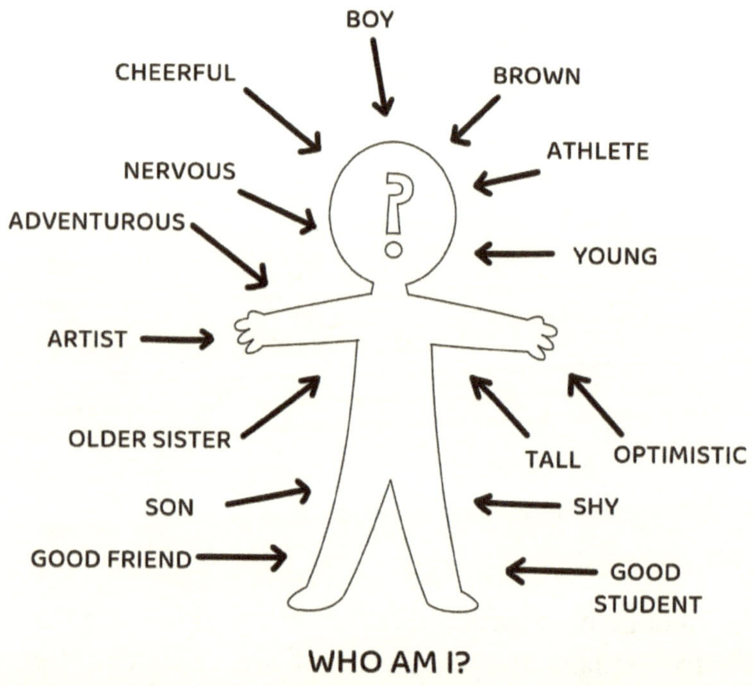

–But Mom, I'm Sophie, when I say that, everyone understands me, everyone knows who I am –she said.

—Yes, child, but do you really know who you are? From a young time they teach us to describe ourselves in that way, so that's what we're used to do, but we're more than just a series of data. Actually, with all those adjectives we create a «character», it's like building a doll with different leftovers that we keep on getting better as we grow but, is that character what we are? The answer is no, we are not those adjectives with which we describe each other; you are not your name, your age, nor your hair color, not even that character we've built with all those words. I'll explain something very ancient to you.

Her mother moved the chair closer so that Sophie could see the computer screen. Where an image of a theatre's ruins could be seen.

—In the Ancient Greece, —she began to explain—, as there was no television, people went to the theatre. Performances were made in an enclosure built with outdoor stones and in the center there was an area of land that was the stage. Since it ended up being such a popular show, a lot of people attended. But, what was going on? It was outdoors and with so many people that nothing could be heard, so they invented masks that they used as a speaker. The actors put the mask on their faces and when they spoke you could hear much better what they were saying. The interesting thing about this story is the name of the masks, they were called «PERSONA» which means «where sounds go through», and so our word «person» was created in those theaters.

—Why do we use such an antique word? —asked Sophie.

—All the terms we use come from ancient words, and it is very interesting to see their origin, to understand their deep meaning, as in the case of the word «person». When we say we are a person, we refer to our character, as if we were wearing a mask to perform in a theater. But now that you know it, you can realize that behind the person there is someone holding the mask, and there, is where we really are.

–Mom, so, if I only know my characteristics, how can I know who really I am? –Asked Sophie.

–That's the question I expected you to ask, the same question that many philosophers have asked themselves in all ages. Do you want to know my favourite philosopher's answer?

–Of course!! –Sophie replied proud of such an important question she had asked herself.

–Socrates said, «Know yourself». This message seems very simple. Socrates was like that, he said things very simply, but it's a phrase you must remember because you're going to use it so many times and it's so true that it's worth to keep in mind.

Sophie at that moment couldn't completely understand that such a simple concept could be important, but she decided to trust what her mother told her and memorized the phrase.

–«Know yourself» means that the answers are in you, you must investigate to know. Would you like to investigate, Sophie?

–Yes, but I don't know how –answered Sophie as she raised her shoulders.

–I propose two exercises, do you dare? –asked her mother as a challenge.

–Yes, what do I have to do? –replied Sophie as she leapt up into military mode.

–First you have to get to know your mask, –said her mother–, becoming familiar with your character and, from there, you can find out what else you are. I suggest you to write ten sentences which start with I AM...

1. I am	___________________
2. I am	___________________
3. I am	___________________
4. I am	___________________
5. I am	___________________
6. I am	___________________
7. I am	___________________
8. I am	___________________
9. I am	___________________
10. I am	___________________

Sophie ran towards her room. She had writing material there and she thought it would be better to do the exercise alone. When she started writing, she realized that searching for words that described her wasn't as easy as it seemed. She took a hand mirror that she had on her desk and started describing herself aloud: I'm a girl, I've got brown hair, I'm tall, I'm thin... She could do a quick exercise if she simply represented her appearance, but she decided to go a little further and thought of the words that best defined her way of being and her personality. The exercise required a lot of sincerity because not everything that defined her was positive. Sophie showed herself her bravery and gradually filled in the ten blanks she had created in a notebook.

After a while, she appeared through the door holding her notebook and feeling satisfied.

–Have you already got it? –asked her mother. Here you can see what your character is like, which features it has, and knowing your character will always be useful to you. Then I'll explain you why. Well, that would be the first step; the second is to know who's behind the mask and in order to know that we need to be aware of a very important thing. WHAT MAKES YOU VIBRATE? –said her mother.

Sophie looked attentively at her awaiting for the instructions about the second step.

–This question is going to take longer than the first exercise –said her mother–. We are trained to answer the question «Who are you?». It's easy, we've answered that question since we started talking, but how many times have they asked you, what makes you vibrate? —said her mother.

—I think it's the first time —replied Sophie.

—In this second step I'm going to suggest that you write down three things, the three things that make you vibrate, with which you feel really good, free, authentic, vital, with energy... —added her mother as she encouraged her to do her homework.

1. It makes me vibrate	_____________
2. It makes me vibrate	_____________
3. It makes me vibrate	_____________

Sophie disappeared for a while, the exercise forced her to look inside herself, to ask questions that she could only answer and she still had the feeling that the answers were not within her grasp.

She searched in her memories for moments when she had felt really happy; she thought of her birthdays, her vacation, the family, of those moments that her memory had described as the best. She finally realized that her best experiences had some sensations in common. At that moment, she did not quite know how to call those sensations, but she did know that they were moments when she connected with her authentic being, where she did not feel that she was wearing any masks that protected her, because there was no threat.

When she finished the exercise, she went back to her mother's. She had her three sentences and showed them to her waiting for approval. Her mother looked at the sentences and embraced her with great tenderness. And she said:

—Now that you've done that research on yourself, don't you think you know yourself a little better? We can say that you know a little more about your character and what your essence is.

–Yes, ok, I like it, I've never thought about it in that way –said Sophie, adding: –I don't like the character, it's better to think who I really am.

–Yes, Sophie, you're absolutely right –said her mother–, but you must know that the character is not bad at all, on the contrary, we need to be a character in order to interact with the world. What's more, we don't just have one character.

–How? Are there more? Where are they? –Asked Sophie, who was bewildered.

–Yes, okay, I don't want to confuse you –said her mother with a smile. We have a «main» character which is often called PERSONALITY, but in fact, we are many characters. When you talk to me or dad you are a daughter, with your friends you are a friend, with your teachers you are a student, and by the way, very responsible, more than at home...! –said her mother ironically, and she went on–. Have you noticed that you are yourself but with tiny differences? You are not the same person at home, at school, in the doctor or you're your grandparents. It is what we call ROLES, in each situation our main character takes on a role, the son's, grandson's, brother's, friend's role... and the roles will expand as you expand your world. Each of those roles will have a slightly different mask.

–Huufff, well now that you are saying it, it's true, I am not always the same person–confessed Sophie, smiling–. What a mess!

–It's actually easier than it looks like, the character and roles are necessary, they're good. When we talk to our teacher we need them to do their teaching role and to guide us. We all know that with their friends, teachers will not be the same as in class.

–Mom, having so many roles aren't going to confuse us? –asked Sophie.

–There's the key Sophie, it's easy for us to get confused –said her mother–. The important thing is to distinguish what the character is and what our authentic being is, because what we are besides the character is what will give us freedom to develop our being, it is our true being. That's why you've done the exercise in two parts, the first part helps you see the character and the second part makes you visible who you really are.

That night Sophie went to bed early. She was thoughtful; she lied down in her bed and looked at the ceiling of her room for a long time. She imagined a large Greek theatre full of people dressed in white tunics and where there was a great din. There were actors wearing masks of different shapes and colors, and at every word the audience excitedly applauded. He imagined the main actor sitting on a bench, saying through his mask, «know yourself».

Before going to sleep Sophie's mother passed through her daughter's bedroom and saw that she was peacefully sleeping. She was surprised how fast her little Sophie was growing up and smiled at the thought she asked herself the same questions at her age.

2
TO HAVE

The next morning Sophie got up early to go to school. When she said goodbye to her mother, she saw that she had her computer ready to go on with her course notes. Would she have more things to explain to her?

That morning she was a little distracted in class thinking about everything her mother had explained to her about the characters, the masks... She had a sense of unreality. She looked around, saw her classmates speak and tried to imagine what they would look like without their masks. Maybe they showed happy when they were actually sad? It was impossible to know with the naked eye.

When they finished classes Sophie ran out in a rush to her house, eager to keep talking to her mother and find out more things she didn't know. When she got home she went upstairs quickly and found her mother in the kitchen where she was finishing preparing the meal.

–Mom, I wanted to ask you what you wrote this morning while I was at school –said Sophie, watching her mother peeling potatoes.

–For today I have written about to have– replied her mother.

–To have? What do you mean? –said Sophie.

–To have is the opposite of to be –replied her mother.

–Ohhh, then the «not to be» that Hamlet said is to have. Isn't it, Mom? –asked Sophie, intrigued.

–That's right, daughter –replied her mother–, we could say that our dilemma is about to be or to have.

–Can you explain to me why to have is the opposite of to be? I don't get it –said Sophie.

–Well, I warn you that this is also a long story –said her mother–. As we learned yesterday, people adopted roles that determine our behavior in front of others, we have seen that we have an essence that guides us towards what makes us vibrate. But not only by doing what we like we will be able to survive in the world, but we need to have resources: a place to live, food to feed ourselves... in short, money. This brings us into the great dilemma: if we want to be, that is, to do what makes us vibrate, or if we want to have, that is, to focus on getting a salary and living with the comforts we desire. This is not to say that we cannot achieve both, but many times we must choose between being or having. Have you heard the phrase «money doesn't give happiness»?

–Yes, I've heard it and I think people have to do what makes them vibrate. That's what's important, we talked about it yesterday –replied Sophie.

—Well, daughter, that's what you usually say, but that decision actually comes at such a high price that many people aren't willing to pay for it —her mother said.

—What price is that? —asked Sophie.

—The price is poverty —replied her mother. Very few people will choose to be happy if it means to be poor. But stop! Before you say anything, I'll tell you do not have to be unhappy. In fact, there are a lot of options, and if you want, I'm going to explain them to you.

—Yes, Mom, because the way you said it sounded really badly —said Sophie.

Her mother looked at her smiling and seeing Sophie's father arrive added:

—Now go and lay the table. It's time to eat.

During the meal they talked about «to have» and Sophie's father explained something that had happened to a workmate.

—Mark won a lot of money in the lottery —said his father—, and we were all very happy for him, he quit his job and moved into a luxurious house on the outskirts of Barcelona. One day I met him by chance and the first thing that surprised me was his gray hair, when he worked with me he had a black mane that was everyone's envy. After greeting us I asked him how his life as rich was going, and with a sad look he explained that the lottery had ruined his life. It had been a disaster, he had fought with his family, because they kept asking him for money. As he was not working he had lost his good habits and had become too inactive, his wife had abandoned him... an endless misfortune that saddened me greatly. It's not easy to manage so much money; it's a too heavy burden for some people.

Sophie's mother nodded and added:

—You have to be careful with what you want, because it can be fulfilled. We think we only need money to be happy, but we're very wrong.

After eating, Sophie moved closer to her mother and asked:

—What have you chosen, Mom?

–Today I'm going to eat strawberry yoghurt – replied her mother absent-mindedly as she looked at where the desserts were–. Can I have one?

Sophie laughed and said:

–No, mom, I mean to choose between to be or to have.

Sophie's mother looked at her and also laughed.

–Before answering that question, you have to know what to have means. We relate to having with money –she continued saying–, and money has been so important, since its inception in human history, that it has caused wars, deaths, abuses of power… That's why we now see money as evil, but in fact, we all need money to live, to meet our basic needs.

–What do you mean by «basic», are not all needs equal? –asked Sophie.

–Well, since you're asking, I'm going to explain it to you –replied her mother. There are different types of needs. A well-known American psychologist put those types in order and built a pyramid. Hmmm, I believe I have a drawing around here, I'll show you.

–A pyramid? What does that have to do with what we're talking about?

–Now you'll understand –replied her mother as she searched out in her computer files–. Here it is, look: Maslow's Pyramid. I'll tell you why Maslow used this figure. You see, to build a pyramid you have to start from the base. Until it isn't complete you can't put the pieces on the top, can you? Have you ever tried it? —she asked.

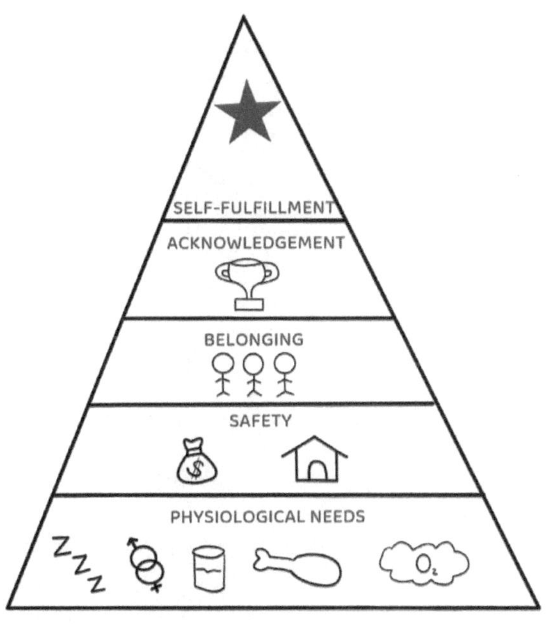

—Yes, I once built a pyramid with letters, but they all fell down —replied Sophie.

—Well, the same thing happens here. But we don't want our pyramid to fall over, so we have to strongly build it. If you look at the drawing you will see that the base of the pyramid are the **physiological needs**, that is, what we need to live, starting by the air and followed by water and food. Then, we also need to go to the bathroom, sleep and from a certain age there are sexual needs. The basis of human life is to stay alive and healthy. It is logical, isn't it?

—Yes, though I've never stopped to think about it —she said.

—Yes, Sophie, you haven't stopped to think about it, but many adults don't think about it either and they don't have a good base in their pyramid. It's hard to build something without that part, and a problem at the base supposes other problems in the higher layers.

—How do I know if I have a good base in my pyramid? —asked Sophie, worried.

—If you want, we can do an exercise. Do you dare? —she challenged her again.

–Of course, I do –replied Sophie–. I also want to build a well-mad pyramid so it doesn't fall like my cards. I didn't like to spend too much time making such a tall tower and then it would fall down without knowing why. It was a disappointment.

–Well, let's do a table to see what your weaknesses may be when you take care of your physiological needs. We're not going to include sexuality because it's not your turn yet, but if you do this exercise again in the future you can include it.

Need	Question	YES/NO
Breathe	Are you aware of your breathing?	
	Do you practice relaxation techniques?	
Drink	Do you often drink water?	
	Do you drink 2 liters of water a day?	

Eat	Do you have a balanced diet?	
	Do you have 5 pieces of fruit or vegetables a day?	
Exercise	Do you play sports at least 3 days a week?	
	Do you walk every day for at least 20 minutes?	
Sleep	Is it hard to get up in the morning?	
	Do you sleep at least 7 hours a day?	
Bathroom	Do you go to the bathroom once a day?	
	Do you often suffer from diarrhea or constipation?	

Sophie went to her room to fill in the questionnaire. After a few minutes she returned a little discouraged.

–Have you already finished it? –asked her mother.

—Yes, but I thought I had a good pyramid and I realize I don't care about my base —she said with a worrying face.

—Sophie, you're still a girl and you don't need to pay so much attention to these things, because you have your parents looking after you —explained her mother—, but it's worth knowing that it's important to have good habits for the future, that's why I tell you to eat vegetables, to go for a bike ride... in order to have good manners. Now, you have to think about what went wrong in the test to improve it little by little, that's all.

—Yes, Mom, it's better to know what I have to improve than to know nothing —she said raising her arm in a sign of strength.

—Well, Sophie —said her mother—, don't think this ends here, the pyramid has more floors. Do you want to know what other needs we have?

—Sure, Mom.

—Okay, but now you have to go back to school, we'll have to find out when you get back.

In the afternoon, when she went out from school, Sophie stayed talking to her friends for a while, she loved being with them. They had to do a group job and took advantage of the good day to stay in the park to organize what part of the work was left to each of them. She came home very happy.

–Hello! –said Sophie when she opened the door–. I'm home.

–Hello, daughter –said her mother while she approached her to give her a hug. She added: –We're all home safely now.

–Why do you say that Mommy? –asked Sophie.

–Because I was thinking about the second floor of the pyramid, the **need of security** –replied her mother–. When you walked through the door you said «I'm home», and although you probably haven't noticed, you've given a sigh and relaxed.

–Now that you say it, it is like that. Every time I come home I feel that way; for example, I love taking off my shoes, it makes me feel like I'm resting.

–That's right, Sophie –said her mother–, when you walk into the house and you relax, you're covering your security need, being in a place where you can lower your alerts and tensions, where you can stop monitoring for any danger, it's instinctive. Just like you take off your shoes that protect your feet, you take off your mental protection and that's why you feel relaxed.

–So, is that pyramid floor okay? –asked Sophie, cheerful.

–Yes, child, you have that need covered and when you have a house and a security you can build the next floor on top.

–Which is the next floor?

–Maslow called it the **need of affiliation** – replied her mother–, which means the need to have friends, to belong to a group, to engage with others affectionately.

–Ah –exclaimed Sophie–, today when I left school I stayed talking to my friends and I felt great.

–That's right, Sophie, just as you have to take care of your health to have a good basis in life, you also have to take care of friends to feel good, because we have that need, even if we don't risk our lives as we do at the base. But once we are healthy and safe, then we also need to have friends and have a good time.

–That's my favorite level –said Sophie with a broad smile.

–I don't know if you'll feel the same way when you see the next levels. The higher in the pyramid the better, the more of being, what makes you vibrate, do you remember?

–Oh, I hadn't thought of it that way, there are still two levels left, right?

–Exactly –replied her mother–. After membership we go up to the level of recognition's necessity. Do you remember the pyramid's drawing, which on that section there was cup drawn?

—Yes.

—Imagine somebody gives you a prize, how would you feel?

—The truth is that it's an amazing feeling; I'd feel better even than chatting with my friends. You were right, Mom, the higher the better.

—So the last level is the best, it's called **self-realization** —said her mother—, and it means that you develop your potential, your essence, what makes you feel, what makes you shine like a star.

Sophie breathed a sigh.

—But don't forget that if you want to reach the top of the pyramid you need the previous floors —

said her mother–, and to get up there you have to work on building a good basis as well as the intermediate levels.

–One question, Mom, you said that at the top there is the being, so at the bottom of the pyramid is having?

–Exactly, daughter, you ask really good questions–, her mother acknowledged. She also added: –Now you won't be able to think that having is a bad thing, will you? Do you realize that we need to have to be able to be?

–I understand now–replied Sophie.

When Sophie went up to her bedroom to do her homework, she stayed there for a while looking at the things she had there. She thought there were a lot of things she didn't really need and made the decision to clean up to preserve what really mattered, so she could leave a little more space to be.

«Happy is the man who can make a living
by his hobby»
GEORGE BERNARD SHAW

3
VOCATION AND PROFESSION

That morning Sophie appeared just after getting up through the kitchen door, still wearing her pajamas with a teddy bear drawn at the height of her belly and her hair was gracefully disheveled. Her mother, who was busy preparing breakfast, looked at her and hid a laugh when she saw her bangs lifted up, but told her nothing not to irritate her: the girl was beginning to be in an age in which any comment about her appearance could become the drama of the day. She was so funny that it made her want to hug her.

The first rays of sunshine entered through the window creating a warm and very pleasant light and smelled of toast and chamomile infusion: the home odor.

–Good morning, Sophie. How was your night's sleep? –asked her mother.

–All right, but yesterday I went to sleep thinking about what I'd be when I grow up, and with everything you've taught me these days, I'm a little confused. I'd like to see my future so I don't have to decide.

–Oh! Well, I'm sorry, I don't want to confuse you –said her mother–, but I can explain something that can help you a little bit. Would you like it?

–I'd like to.

–Go and get dressed, comb your hair and I'll tell you while we have breakfast.

Sophie didn't take long to get ready; she was hungry and in two minutes she was already back to the kitchen. Her mother was surprised. Once at the table and with the steaming breakfast, the lesson began:

–Sophie –her mother said–, you're going to have to decide what you want to study soon, to learn a profession. It's important to consider what you would like to do when you grow up. I'm going to show you a picture and I want you to look at it carefully and tell me what you see.

Sophie looked at her mother's laptop, where she saw a simple black-and-white drawing, in which two people appeared. And then she got herself ready to describe what she was seeing:

—I can see a boy with a cell phone, a watch, sunglasses and next to him a poor boy with broken clothes —replied Sophie.

—Anything else? Her mother asked. Look at their faces.

—Oh yes! The rich boy is sad and the poor boy is happy.

—Can you imagine why? Her mother asked.

—I think so; the rich kid is the one who belong to the "to have". He owns things, but he doesn't have the joy to be; whereas the poor child does what he likes and is happy, but doesn't earn money to buy clothes.

–Perfect Sophie, that's right. We were talking about being and having and in this drawing, we can see the differences.

–So, Mom, do I have to choose between one of the two options? –asked Sophie in a concerned tone.

–No, not at all –her mother clarified–, this drawing represents both extremes, but in real life things are not black or white, they are gray.

–I've heard that phrase at school, but I don't really understand it –said Sophie. I don't understand when you say things are gray.

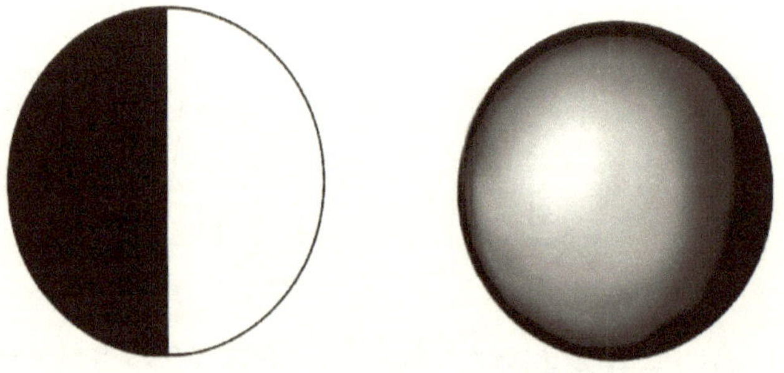

At that time, Sophie's mother, who had finished breakfast, arranged to prepare Sophie's and her brother Jan's sandwich to take him to school.

–Well, daughter –her mother said –, the phrase refers to what we've just talked about. When you say something, we tend to go to extremes. For example, if you eat a sandwich, you'll say it's good, if you've liked it, or you'll say it's bad, if you haven't liked it. But the reality is that in the continuum between the good and the bad there are many nuances and we could say that the good or the bad at 100 percent does not exist, because you can always try a better sandwich than the previous one. So it is usually said that something is not black or white, referring to the extremes, but that the reality is gray, between one color and the other. If you watch life with extremes you miss the important thing, because the important thing is in the nuances. If you remain at the extremes you're not in the truth; you're doing things simply, like a button that can only be on or off. You don't need to simplify things to understand them, people have the ability to think and value thousands of possibilities.

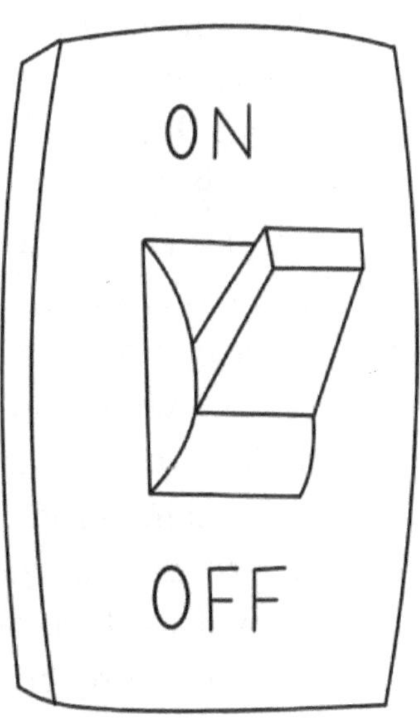

–I think I understand you, but I want to let you know that your sandwiches are delicious–, she said with a roguish smile.

–I already knew that –said her mother. I'm a great cook, it's a good thing you've noticed.

–Well, don't go too far either, Mom –said Sophie mockingly.

–Daughter, I like cooking, but it's not my vocation –her mother replied, returning to the conversation's topic.

–Vocation? What do you mean? –Sophie asked.

–I still have a lot of things to explain to you. We have been talking about being, about having and about the needs of people who encompass aspects of being and aspects of having. Now you know that it's important to know your being and also how to develop it while meeting your needs. When you decide what job you want to do, you're going to think about these two things: what you like and what can give you money. We will call the «to be» VOCATION, that is, what makes you vibrate, what you would do for pleasure, not for money. And then for the «to have» we will call it PROFESSION, that is, what you would do to have a salary and live covering your needs. However, attention! if you imagine a line where we have at one end the profession and at the other end the vocation, we will find many intermediate points, where the nuances are countless. We're going to make it simple therefore we'll summarize it in five options.

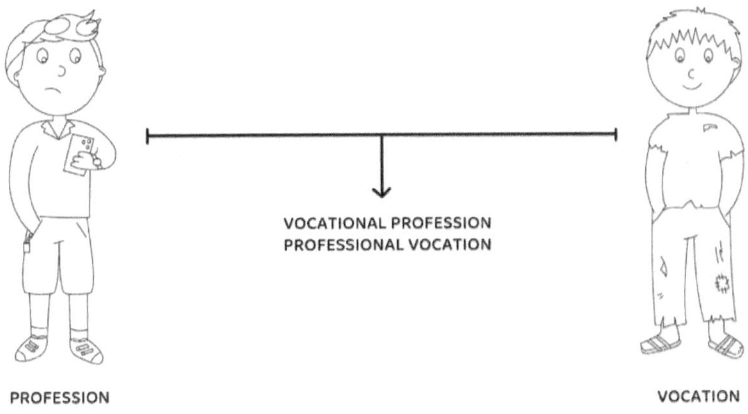

- PROFESSION WITHOUT VOCATION: we make money, but we don't like our job.

- VOCATION WITHOUT PROFESSION: we do what we like, but we don't earn money.

- VOCATIONAL PROFESSION: we have a job to make money that we finally like.

- PROFESSIONAL VOCATION: we do what we like as well as we also earn money.

- NO PROFESSION NOR VOCATION: we don't make money nor we like what we do. This option doesn't make any sense, although you'd be surprised at the people who can choose it. It's the worst option by far.

Sophie watched attentively to her mother's explanation.

–Which do you think are the best options out of the five we've seen? her mother asked.

–Three and four, because they have the advantages of both vocation and profession – replied Sophie.

–That's right, daughter. Doesn't it seem so complicated now? These two options are the most powerful to have a full life. The first two make you pay a price: vocation without profession can make you happy but poor, instead the profession without vocation can make you rich but unhappy.

–Mom which of the two options is better? Have a professional vocation or vocational profession? – Sophie asked.

And then she laughed after she had managed to say that complicated tongue-twister. Her mother, passed on by her daughter's guffaws, took a few minutes to answer. After the laugh attack, she said:

–Both are equally good because they have a balance between both aspects. If you look at the drawing you will see that they are just in the middle of the two ends.

–Yes, I can see it, they're actually the same, even if they start differently– said Sophie.

—I will tell you with another example: imagine that vocation is a heart and profession are the feet. For the boy to work, he needs both parts: having a heart that drives him to move, and two feet to hold on. That's who we are. —She also added: —Now, think there are hearts with big feet and hearts with small feet, and also small and big hearts.

Sophie imagined hearts with feet of different sizes.

—How fun! —She said, laughing.

She thought she wanted a big heart, but her feet would also have to be big, as she had learned that a good base is necessary to build on it in a solid way.

That morning, breakfast was so long that Sophie was almost late for school. Mother and daughter lost sight of time as they were speaking. When they realized what time it was, Sophie picked up all her stuff and rushed out. Once at school, sitting on her desk, she took her notebook and set out to draw the hearts with feet she had imagined before.

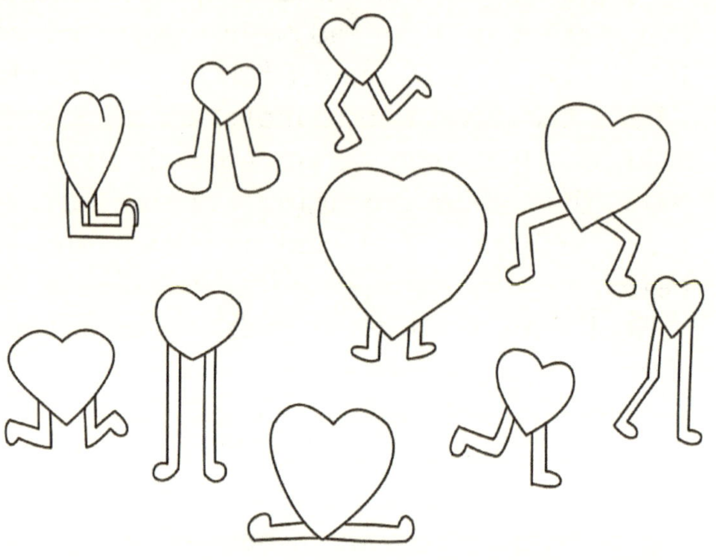

4
FUTURE

The following morning Sophie got up earlier than usual. She was going to a day trip with the school and she was nervous. She was preparing the backpack, the canteen and the other things she had been told at school. Everything was about to have a great day.

When she came down the stairs, she saw in horror that there was a great storm.

–Oh no! –she exclaimed to herself.

–Good morning, Sophie, it looks like the trip is cancelled, look at such a terrible storm! –she exclaimed.

–I see –Sophie said disappointingly. I was very excited about this excursion, I had it all prepared.

–I know, daughter, sometimes our plans are affected by the emerging.

–The emerging? What does that mean? –asked Sophie curiously.

–Lately, you ask me a lot of questions, it will be that you're getting older! –said her mother as she gave her daughter a big hug–. I'll answer you, just sit down.

Mother and daughter sat on the couch, covered the tops with a blanket and looked outside. Through the window they saw the dark sky, the strange shapes of the clouds, and warned how the relentless wind moved the trees from side to side and caused the rain to hit the windowpanes.

–People have mental schemes, that is, we make representations in our minds of everything –her mother said–. Think for a moment about what your mind created when you were told you were going on a day trip today.

Sophie kept a little while thinking and then said:

–In my mind, I had imagined that I was getting on the coach, chatting with my friends during the journey and we arrived at the school camp house. There were some instructors there that took us to do some activities, we participated in some climbing circuits and we threw on giant zip lines. Everything was a lot of fun, and I was very excited to do the activities that they explained to us...

—That's what people do —her mother said—, it's like if another world exists in our minds, and when the time comes true, it may or may not look like our representation. That you make a representation in your mind is good; it allows you to plan what you'll do, predict problems and solutions, and adapt to unforeseen events faster. But it also creates an expectation, and you have to be careful, because our representation does not take into account anything that might happen for no apparent reason, such as raining and canceling the tour.

—That's why I feel sad —said Sophie—, because I hoped everything was going to be all right today.

–Exactly, and that happens to us throughout our lives. We can make plans for the future and sometimes unexpected things happen.

–Then planning is only to make us feel sad! –Sophie exclaimed.

–No, it's not, and now you'll see why –her mother explained–. In life, we have to take a direction, plan what we want for ourselves, and we will call that a planned future. It's what sets out our course like we were a ship.

–Yes –Sophie said, looking out of the window–, but there are a lot of storms.

—That's right, Sophie, along the journey we're going to run into storms, ones will be bigger and other smaller ones, which can change our course. That's what we're going to call the emerging future.

At that very moment a great thunder sounded outside, and Sophie, scared, pounced on her mother.

—We can't control storms, but we can know they exist and we can avoid they make us feel scared or sad. It's better to let them go by and then go back to set our course towards our destiny.

Sophie's mother paused to observe her daughter's reaction.

—There are such big storms —she said—, that they make us completely change our course, they affect us so much, they make us want something different in life. We call those storms THE BIG. There are people who call it destiny.

—Okay, Mom, everything you're saying is alright, but the truth is that I'm not going on a day trip today, and preparing the backpack with all the stuff was useless —Sophie said a little annoyed.

—That's right, Sophie, the reality is different — her mother said. And she added: —The real future is the intersection of the planned future and the emerging future. What's going to happen is not really going to be what we've imagined, but it's not going to be fate either, but both things are going to add up; therefore, it is useful to plan, because otherwise, you will be completely in the hands of fate.

Sophie closed her eyes to concentrate on what her mother was telling her, trying to imagine various possibilities, as if she could see several dimensions at the same time: what she had planned, what it had emerged and what was actually happening.

–Sometimes the most important thing is not to reach the goal, but to have goals, motivations and illusions, and finally, although you don't reach them, you will have grown along the way.

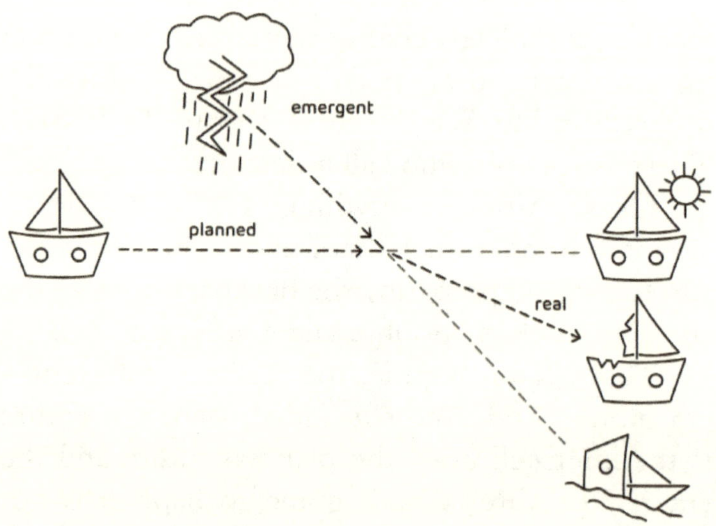

–Do you know Ulysses, the main character of «The Odyssey»? –her mother asked.

—No —replied Sophie as she raised her shoulders.

—You must know that work, it's very important. It is a Greek poem written by Homer, which chronicles the adventures of Ulysses, a hero who returns home after the Trojan War.

—The Trojan War I do know it —said Sophie, excitedly—. It was the one in which they built a giant horse and people hid inside. At the end, it turned out to be a trap.

—Exactly —her mother said—, so when the Trojan War ends, Ulysses wants to go back home and it takes him ten years on a long journey full of adventures. Some people say that the Odyssey is the most influential work in history.

Sophie was surprised to realize that she did not know such an important work. She thought she still had a lot to learn and was very happy to be able to rely on her mother.

—Mom —said Sophie—. What does the Odyssey have to do with the future?

—Very good question, daughter —her mother said—. Ulysses' journey is considered a symbol of life, and the adventures that happen to him symbolize the difficulties we may encounter. Do you want me to explain an example?

—Yes —Sophie replied.

—One of the most famous adventures of Ulysses' journey is the one about the mermaids' singing. You see, Ulysses was traveling on a boat with his crew and knowing that they would sail across a place where many ships disappeared because of the mermaids' singing, he asked his crew members to truss him up to the ship's mast. Even though he knew the danger, he was curious to hear that special singing. So, he devised a plan: he ordered the rest of the crew members to cover their ears with wax. He told them not to untie him no matter what happened. When Ulysses heard the mermaids' song he begged to be released, but the sailors were warned and that's how they managed to sail through the mermaids' territories without diverting from their trip.

—What did the sirens do to the sailors they caught? —asked Sophie.

—The sirens' singing were a death trap, they attracted the sailors to them and caused the boats to crash into the rocks, then they killed them and ate them. Actually, they were monsters.

Sophie was surprised that such an ancient book could contain such an exciting story. He had liked the story of mermaids eating sailors and thought that when he had time he would read the adventures of Ulysses. She was curious to know more stories.

—Alright —her mother said—. What do you think mermaids can symbolize?

Sophie didn't quite know what to answer, she wasn't used to looking for symbols, she found it somewhat difficult. After a short silence, she raised her shoulders indicating she had no answer.

—The mermaids' songs —her mother said—, symbolize the pleasant and convincing words we like to hear, but which hide some deception. In fact, there is the expression «mermaids' singing» when someone wants to deceive you.

—Sure —Sophie said, understanding what her mother was explaining to her.

—What you have to learn from this —her mother said—, is that life is a journey to a destination that you choose and where you will encounter difficulties, like storms or sirens. Those difficulties are actually adventures, which are the ones that are going to make you grow.

That day, on the way to school and with the umbrella in hand, Sophie reflected on her future. She had never really thought about planning a destination and what course to take. If she felt so discouraged by not going to the day trip, how would she feel about other types of unforeseen events? Maybe she should start planning and thinking about how to overcome some obstacles. At that moment, she met a classmate, who also seemed as disappointed as she was as they couldn't go to the excursion.

–Today there was no rain forecast –complained the girl. I just looked at it on my cell phone. This wasn't part of my plans.

As she uttered these words, the girl inadvertently stepped on a puddle full of water which soaked her up, and this made her snort indignantly.

–The thing is, we haven't taken into account the emerging –said Sophie distractedly.

–What? –asked her partner.

–No, nothing, my stuff –said Sophie, sighing as she grabbed her friend's arm.

And they kept on walking to school as they lamented the unexpected rain.

«To be aware of limitations
is already to be beyond them»
Hegel

5
FEAR

It was Saturday and there was no school. Sophie got up early in order to read a little bit before breakfast, but when she saw her mother typing in her laptop in the living room she went down to talk to her. She had a question to ask her.

–Mom, good morning –she said–, there's one thing I'm worried about. I'm thinking about what we talked about and that I will have to choose what I want to be when I grow up, but how do I know I'm not wrong?

–Good morning! daughter, it's normal you ask yourself this question –her mother replied–. Whenever we're going to do something new, that we don't control, we're going to be afraid. Fear is part of change.

–Yes, but isn't there a way to choose properly? –the girl asked.

–Yes –her mother said–, I've already explained you what aspects you need to take into account to choose. However, no matter how much you think about the choice, there's nothing for sure, there's always going to be fear, and despite fear you have to act, take a risk.

Sophie was pensive for a moment. Her mother observed her, and seeing that she was worried, she thought it was a good time to explain some things to her.

–Sophie –said her mother–, if you have a moment, I'd like to explain something to you.

–Yes, I have time, it's Saturday.

–Well –her mother said –. I would like to explain that people are not frightened of doing the same thing every day because we have the feeling that we control the situation and that we know what is going to happen. That's fine, because we're calm and happy. That's called THE COMFORT ZONE. But if we always do the same thing, we will not evolve; if we do not go through a moment of fear in order to do something different, we will not learn, nor grow.

Sophie imagined herself lying down on the couch looking at her mobile phone, it was nice.

–Around the comfort zone –her mother continued–, we found the LEARNING AREA, that is, when we do new things, when we learn something we didn't know when we change our way to go to school, when we try a meal that we thought we didn't like... In that space we're going to do things we're not used to, and from that experience we're going to learn.

Sophie thought of that day she talks to the whole school. It was the first time she spoke in front of that amount of people, and she had a really bad time; she got very nervous and her voice was shaking, but once everything had happened, she was satisfied and really happy.

–I understand that life is very boring if you always do the same thing –Sophie said–. But I'm afraid of being wrong about something that's going to last a lifetime.

–That's right –her mother said–, you're not thinking about leaving the comfort zone, you're thinking of leaving the learning zone.

–Is there another area? Which one? –Sophie asked very curiously.

–After the learning area –her mother said with a certain sense of suspense–, there is the PANIC ZONE. What's called the abyss.

The word «panic» made Sophie shiver all over her body. She imagined a dark trench with terrible monster sounds and thought no one would go to that area voluntarily.

–Beyond the learning area –her mother said–, is where there are fears and anxiety due to novelty. There's a place we won't even want to get close. That area is brand new, we don't know anything about that place. And as you must know, what we do not know is frightening. If you pay attention, many movies use the «panic zone» to create adventure stories. There is usually a protagonist who enters the forbidden place to explore the unknown. And he usually learns a lesson there.

–So, what lies ahead for me in the future… is it something called a panic zone? That doesn't exactly cheer me up, Mom! –Sophie said, with her eyes wide open.

–Yes, that's right –her mother said–. But you should know that the panic zone is also the MAGIC AREA where extraordinary things can happen. Even though, it's up to you that the territory becomes terrifying or magical. Remember, you don't know what's in there, you just know there's a big question waiting for you. Why there must be something wrong if we don't know what's there? Here is where we could say that we must dare to enter into the unknown, that is: «Dare to dream». I propose a very simple exercise. Could you write down what things you do or you would do within each of the development zones: comfort zone, learning zone and magic zone?

–I dare –Sophie said.

Sophie took advantage that they were alone in the living room to stay and do the exercise there. He went to get her notebook and drew a table with three columns.

COMFORT ZONE	LEARNING AREA	MAGIC AREA

She spent some time doing the exercise. She started considering of what she did on a daily basis; she realized her routine was comfortable, but that it did not make her vibrate. When she wrote activities where she learned new things, she was more nervous, but at the same time they were things she did with great enthusiasm. When she came to the magical zone she began to dream, she imagined great things, perhaps even unattainable things, who could know?

–In order to get into the magic zone, you have to do a good job first –her mother said–, you have to do what Socrates said, do you remember?

–Yes, I do remember, «know yourself» –Sophie said, glad to know the answer–. You already told me I had to remember this phrase and that I would use it again.

–Well, before you enter that area –her mother said–, you must acknowledge your fears, identify them in order to fight them. Everyone is afraid of something: fear of failure, fear of ridicule, fear of what they will say... If you recognize what you are afraid of, you will be able to face it with courage.

–How are fears combated? –Sophie asked.

–Well, the first thing is to identify them, as we said. Then you can work on them in different ways, but, for example, you can think about what's the worst that can happen and when you realize that the worst that can happen isn't that severe either, fear gradually loses strength.

–I see –Sophie said.

–Sometimes fear is worse than what you are afraid of, I don't know if you know what I mean – her mother said–. It's what is called «fear of fear». If you don't know what you're afraid of, you can fall into that trap.

Sophie nodded thoughtfully and said:

–Fear of fear! how do we get complicated sometimes, don't we?

–Yes, daughter –her mother said–. The human mind is a real mystery.

That afternoon Sophie was thinking of Socrates' phrase. She thought that man already knew everybody has fears and it was important to know them. «So, since ancient times people have had to learn what fear is» –she thought to herself.

Sophie was beginning to understand the importance of that phrase that seemed so simple. She thought it had been used by many people since ancient times, and now it was her turn. The message had come to her in order to help her on her way of knowing herself.

This made her think that maybe it wasn't so bad to be afraid; it meant she was in a growing area and somehow, she wasn't alone with her fear of making mistakes. These thoughts encouraged her and she suddenly got up from her chair, went to get her notebook and started writing down what scared her and what was the worst thing that could happen to her if she was wrong.

Gradually, he realized that making a mistake was not the end either and she could even learn something along the way.

6
UNCONSCIOUS

That morning, Sophie showed up earlier than usual.

–Good morning, Sophie, what is that face? –her mother asked when she saw the girl coming down the stairs looking like she hadn't slept a wink.

–I had a horrible dream tonight –she replied–. I dreamed that I was being chased throughout a very strange place, I was running, but I had the feeling that I was not moving forward. There were some gloomy buildings where the doors and windows were dark hollows and you could see something moving inside. Then, I fell into a hole and keep falling, never getting to the bottom.

–Oh, wow –her mother said–, it looks like you've really had a hard time. Your unconscious is telling you something.

–My what? –Sophie asked, without understanding anything.

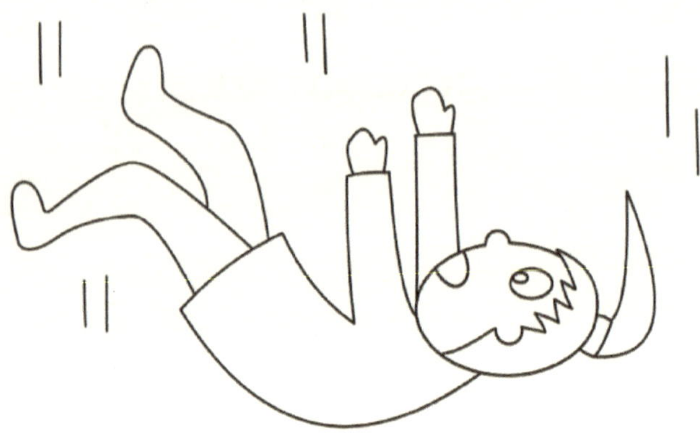

—Your unconscious —her mother repeated—, it is long to explain.

—I want to know who's telling me something! —Sophie said, with great determination.

Her mother looked at her with certain satisfaction as she had all of her daughter's attention, she had to recognize that she was a good student. She knew how to listen and when to ask. Now, she was facing a somewhat complicated subject: the unconscious. She was looking forward to her daughter's reaction, would she be prepared to understand such abstract concepts? She could check it out right away.

—Well, Sophie —she finally said—. People have consciousness, that is, what we «know»: we know who we are, what we think, what we like, what we dislike... don't we?

–Yes, I know myself and, what's more, I know a little more about my character now –Sophie said.

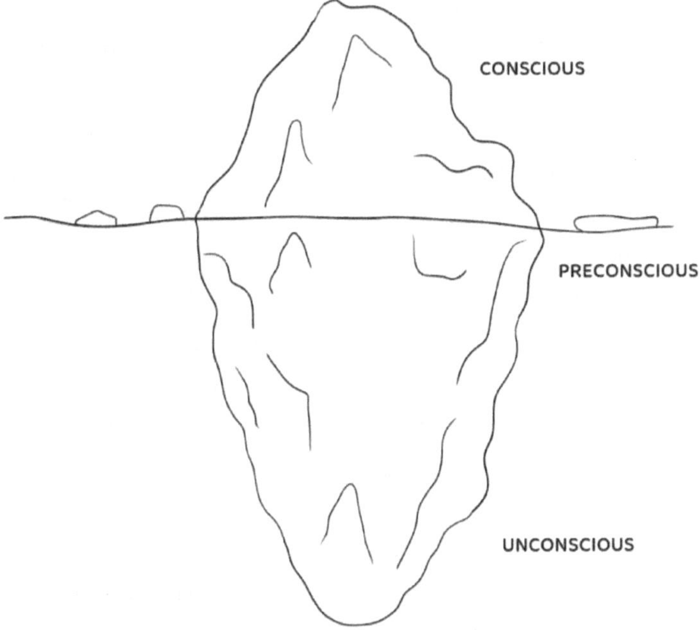

–Exactly, according to the famous psychiatrist Sigmund Freud, there are parts of us that we do not know, he said that the mind is divided into three levels: the conscious, the preconscious and the unconscious. To explain this, he created the «ICEBERG METAPHOR». The conscious is the part of the mind that allows us to be rational; it is totally under our control and everything there is available to us. There are no mechanisms to defend that part, therefore it is the iceberg area that is seen with the naked eye. The preconscious is that part that is shown through water, you can't freely control it, but we could get to see what's there. In this case, making an effort, we would have to overcome some defense mechanisms. The unconscious is the place where desires, passions, repressed memories, primary instincts and impulses are. We will only be able to access this information when we accept it and integrate it as part of us.

Sophie thought about what her mother was explaining to her and remembered that in class they had studied the icebergs. They were masses of floating ice, and a curious fact was that only a ten percent of their total could be seen. That raised a question to her.

–Does this mean we have more hidden than visible things? –she asked and added indignantly: – That is not possible.

–Well, that's right, daughter –her mother replied. There are many more unconscious than conscious things.

–I don't understand how I might have something in my mind and I don't even know it; how does that happen?

–There are many types of unconscious information –her mother replied–. In some cases these are automatic processes of the body itself, such as breathing or heartbeat, and then there is also hidden information for other reasons.

—What reasons can those be? —Sophie asked intriguedly.

—We have said that there is information hidden by the DEFENSE MECHANISMS —her mother replied—. Information we don't know we have. The mind hides it because it sees it as dangerous and wants to protect us.

—But how do you do it? How do you hide things? —Sophie asked.

—I'll explain it to you with an example —her mother replied—. Imagine you're driving and you have an accident. At that moment you go through a lot of fear, so much fear, that your mind collapses. Then your mind chooses to hide that experience in the unconscious so that you can bear it. It's what's called trauma. Some people who have experienced accidents have forgotten them, because the mind has defended them from a suffering they could not bear.

–And is that good or bad? Wouldn't it be nice to know everything that is in our minds? – Sophie asked.

–It's a good thing at first, –her mother replied – . It allows the person to endure something that is painful, but only works for a while. It's going to work as the person evolves and acquires resources to withstand that trauma. There comes a time when defense mechanisms act as brakes for people and it is appropriate to make them aware. For example: in the case of a car accident, it sometimes happens that a person is afraid to get in cars, or to enter closed places and they do not know why.

The unconscious ends up manifesting itself in one way or another.

–What if it doesn't manifest? –Sophie asked–. Something like this has never happened to me.

–One way for the unconscious to manifest is in dreams –her mother replied–. Don't you remember your nightmare anymore? Let me guess what your dream meant: yesterday we talked about the magic zone, and although you liked the idea, there was a moment that it scared you. You denied that fear, as a defense mechanism is the DENIAL. By not accepting fear in you and went to your unconscious, so in your dream appeared that fear denied, like a message from the unconscious. Do you think your dream might mean that? –asked she finally.

–Yes, it makes sense what you say –nodded Sophie–. What should I do?

–Just accept that you're afraid, no one expects you to never be afraid, or to be perfect. So don't ask yourself either. It is important to accept fear in us, it is natural and it is something that makes us alert. Fear is an emotion we need.

–I'll think about it –Sophie said.

Sophie found it very interesting to know that through dreams we can receive valuable information to get to know ourselves. She thought she wanted to know more and asked:

–How many defense mechanisms are there?

–There are many –her mother replied–. They have classified them in many ways and with a lot of names: displacement, dissociation, denial, projection, repression, condensation, rationalization, regression, annulment, reversal, sublimation... Tons of names to describe excuses, forgetfulness, escapes... in this way, they do not to face the truth. If you know them it's entertaining to watch people when they use them.

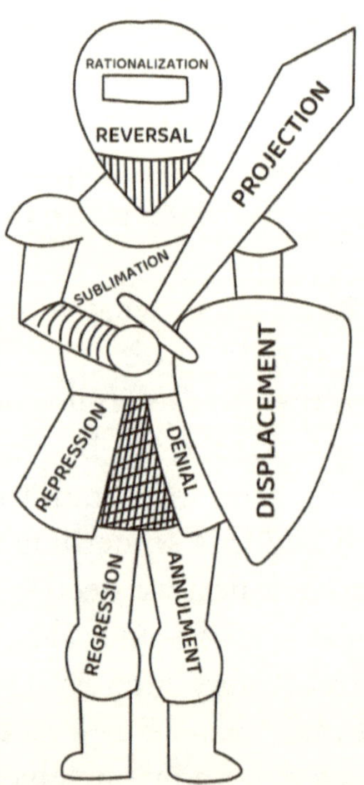

–Can you explain any of them to me? I can't imagine how I can see someone using a defense mechanism.

–Sure, I'll explain a couple of them –her mother replied–. Rationalization, for example, is something we use a lot. When we make a mistake, it is sometimes difficult for us to recognize it was our fault and a mechanism is activated that frees us from it. It's about looking for excuses that aren't our responsibility and so it seems we don't have to suffer.

–Really? Is it that what we do? –Sophie said somewhat incredulously.

–Yes, imagine the next situation –her mother replied–. A girl, named Sophie, doesn't do her maths homework. When he gets to class, instead of saying she didn't do them due to laziness, she looks for a reason to justify why she didn't. But it is not a conscious lie, but she believes what she says: for example, that the exercises were not well explained and she could not do them.

–Oops! –Sophie exclaimed when took the hint.

–I'll give you another example that is also used a lot –her mother added–. It's called displacement. Imagine you have a bad day at school because the teacher scolds you for talking to a classmate in class, and on top of that it's not your fault. You know you can't get mad at the teacher, so you shut up and when you get home, you start yelling at your little brother. You unconsciously move your anger to the teacher to another person, because you unconsciously value that other person is weaker than you.

Sophie was beginning to regret asking that question, she thought sometimes it's not appropriate to know so much.

–Oh! –Sophie said a little embarrassed, and to change the subject she asked: –How can I find out what part of my consciousness is hidden?

–Well –her mother said–, there are different ways to gain in consciousness, for example by analyzing your dreams as I told you before. You can find out a few things, Sigmund Freud said: «*the interpretation of dreams is the royal road to a knowledge of the unconscious activities of the mind*»

When we sleep, our defense mechanisms are deactivated and our minds are free to express what we have in the unconscious.

–But I don't know what dreams mean – Sophie said, as she raised her shoulders.

–If you want to work on your dreams, the first advised thing is to have a notebook on the bedside table to write them down –her mother suggested–. You already know that sometimes we quickly forget them.

Her mother was pensive for a moment, looking for a word in her memory. She didn't remember the name of that tribe that gave great importance to dreams. Suddenly, she said aloud:

–The Senoi! I'll explain something about the Senoi. It is a tribe from an island in Malaysia, which turned out to be known because its people lived very happily and hardly suffered any mental illness. The Senoi were called «the dream people» because they spent a lot of time talking about dreams. Each morning, at breakfast, family members explained what they had dreamed of and the elders told the younger ones how they would have acted in the dream. Then, they would go to the assembly and explain the most important dreams of each family, and the sorcerers would analyze them and seek their meaning. They had a method of solving the problems which arose in dreams. Would you like to know which one it is?

–Sure, can I use it?

–First, I'm going to explain it to you and then you'll tell me if you can use it –her mother clarified and followed the explanation–. The method is based on five points:

- **Face the fears**: when we dream of a danger you have to face it, never run away, you have to stay and fight.

- **Explore in pleasant dreams**: when we dream of something nice, such as flying, we do not have to get carried away by the wind, but you have to explore where we want to go with will.

- **Transform the negative into positive:** when we dream, instead of running away from something we don't like, we have to try to turn it into something positive. For example, in your dream where you fall into the abyss, you should try to guide your fall in order to go somewhere nice.

- **Repair offenses**: when we dream of a fight with someone you know, we should go and talk to that person and if we have offended them, give them a gift to make up for it.

- **Find counselors and guides:** The Senoi advise having a teacher to tell your dreams and helps you deciphering them.

At the end of the explanation, her mother asked her:

—What do you think? Can you use it?

—I think so, would you be my counselor, mommy? —Sophie said, laughing.

Sophie thought that the Senoi method could also be useful in real life: in front of a problem it is better to face it than to run away; facing a new situation you should explore to the end, and besides, seek the positive part of everything, to say sorry when we offend someone and to ask for advice to those who know more than we do.

When it came the time to go to sleep, Sophie left a notebook and a pen ready on her bedside table to write down her dreams as soon as she woke up. However, she was not able to remember anything the next morning.

«Until you make the unconscious conscious,
it will direct your life and you will call it fate»
CARL GUSTAV JUNG

7
ARCHETYPES

That day, Sophie's mother picked her up after the end of school. They had to buy school supplies and headed to the town center. Sophie's friends, who lived in the surrounding area, walked along with them.

–How was the day at school? Sophie's mother asked.

–Well –the girls in unison replied.

–Today was Peace Day and we've had a party where we've dressed up as people from different places –Sophie said.

–Japan has fallen to me –Laia said, one of Sophie's friend–. I love it, Japanese people are so different!

–Yes, people in such faraway places seem very different from us –Sophie's mother said–, but do you know that all people have something have something in common? Something we don't know we have.

–What is it? –the girls asked with a strange face.

–It's called COLLECTIVE UNCONSCIOUS –Sophie's mother said–. There is information that all the people of the world have, but which we are not aware of. Sophie already knows what unconscious means, don't you? Can you explain it to your friends?

Sophie was a little embarrassed in front of her mother and friends. At this moment she remembered that she was not the same person with her mother as with her friends, she had different roles, and this situation made her feel uncomfortable, because she did not know how she should behave. Even though, she tried to explain to her friends what the unconscious was.

–Our mind is like an iceberg –she finally said–, the part we see would be the information we know, that is, the conscious one; on the other hand, there is a large submerged part, which is information that we do not know but that we have within, and that information appears in dreams, in fears...

–Very good daughter –her mother said.

One of Sophie's friends raised her hand to ask to speak, as if she was at school.

–Yes, Annie, would you like to say something? –Sophie's mother asked.

–What is that information? How do you know that everyone in the world has got it? Has anybody asked them? –she asked full of curiosity.

–Good question, Annie –Sophie's mother said –. Not everyone in the world has been asked about. Moreover, if we've said it is hidden information, people would not be able to respond, even if we asked.

The girls, who listened attentively, nodded.

–I'll explain it to you –Sophie's mother said–, this discovery was made by a person named Carl Jung. He traveled all over the world and collected stories from far away, and gradually realized that the same characters appeared everywhere. Even in places that were isolated from everything, whose inhabitants had never communicated with other populations, the information was the same. Then, he made a theory that consists in inheriting that information when people are born.

–But that's not possible, how can you tell some stories if no one has explained them to you? – asked Mary.

–You'll see –said Sophie's mother–, not everything we know we've learned it. Look for example with animals. How does a bee know it has to go to collect to the flowers? Or what shape does a honeycomb have? Every bee in the world builds honeycombs in the same way. Animals also share information with their species.

The girls looked at each other Hesitantly.

–The collective unconscious is formed, among other things, by what Jung called ARCHETYPES, which are like types of personalities, and each person can develop similar behaviors with each other, that is, act in a certain way by influence of those kind of people. Among all the archetypes there is usually a predominant one that dominates our personality and it is good to know which one it is. Why, Sophie? —her mother asked, with a quick look at her.

—Because as Socrates said, you have to know yourself —Sophie replied—, showing that the lesson was well known.

—If you want, girls, let's go to that park for a moment and I will explain to you what the archetypes are. Maybe you can find out which one is yours. Would you like it?

—Yes —the girls shouted excitedly.

They headed to the park, to a triangular corner next to the entrance that had three benches and a fountain. There were some trees around, that created a pleasant, dark shadow. Sophie's mother sat in the center of one of the benches, and instantly was surrounded by the girls who struggled to be closer to the narrator, leaving the floor covered in backpacks launched in a hurry. Once placed, the mother said:

—While it is true that there are many classifications of archetypes, a very common one is that of the twelve basic archetypes. Very summarized, they would be:

- The LOVER: a person who lives with passion, enjoys beautiful things and is very sociable.
- The JESTER: a fun and original person who can't stand boredom.
- The CREATOR: the one who likes novelty, who has great imagination, who is impulsive and messy. This person is the artist.
- The CARER: a sacrificed and protective person of others. This person is calm and generous.
- The EXPLORER: attracted to adventure, this person is restless, idealistic and lives in an eternal quest.
- The RULER: a leading person, who is responsible and controlling, and also suspicious.
- The HERO: a fighting and courageous person. They have great courage and are attracted to conflict. They succeed.
- The ORPHAN: They are a victim, fearful and prudent people. They do not assume responsibilities.
- The INNOCENT: This person is kind and confident. They like peace and are optimistic about problems.

- The MAGICIAN: They are great communicators, attractive people and influencers, sometimes they can be manipulative.
- The OUTLAW: a defiant and disobedient person, but they are often peaceful and quiet in their demands.
- The WISE: a person who enjoys learning. They are lonely and patient, observant and perfectionist.

The girls listened attentively to the description of each of the twelve archetypes, sometimes laughing and commenting about a characteristic or identifying one of them with one of the types.

—Girls, if you want, I can send you a test[1] with a series of questions that will help you find out which archetype influences you the most in your life —Sophie's mother said—. One last thing, each archetype has good characteristics, which we call light, but it also has bad characteristics, which we call shadow. Like everything in life has a good part and a bad part, and it is important to know both parts, even if we do not like the bad too much.

The girls nodded, picked up their backpacks and set out on their way home. The next day, at break time, they commented excitedly about which archetype appeared after doing the test and

---

[1] The test can be found in the annex at the end of the book.

explained to other girls that did not know them what it was about.

8
SHADOW

The next day, Sophie and her mother talked about the archetype test. Sophie explained to her mother that the test had caused a frenzy at school and that girls were passing it to each other and then they were asking for the results. They made lists and statistics on the number of jesters, wise, rulers… in each class. If a child had not taken the test or had not shared the result, there was an evaluating commission which discussed what archetype he or she was, depending on their behavior, and if they lacked information they were asking their closest friends in order to be able to deduce what type they belonged to.

Sophie and her mother laughed at this exaggerated reaction.

—Can you believe the mess that it has formed? —Sophie said.

–I never would have guessed –her mother replied–, but I really like that you talk about things that encourage your classmates to get to know each other a little better at school.

–Mom, there's something I don't understand – Sophie said.

–Tell me, daughter, what is it?

–I don't like what has come out in the negative features, it's not true that I'm like that!

–It's normal, daughter –her mother reassured –, no one likes to recognize their negative things, their shadow. We all have a negative part which makes us human. But you have to recognize it. If we don't, we'll project it onto other people. Can you imagine what the projection is?

After thinking for a moment, she was very excited to have found the answer:

–A defense mechanism –she said excitedly.

–All right, daughter, I see you pay a lot of attention, it makes me very happy –her mother said, full of satisfaction–. That's right, we know that all people have things we don't like, but instead of accepting it we deny it and we usually adjudicate it to someone else, in such a way that we can even criticize that person for anything we do not like. It's said that the person you can't stand is the one who best represents your shadow, so it's worth watching the ones you don't like, don't you think?

–I would never have thought so –Sophie said. The people I don't like are the ones who look the least like me.

–Exactly. It's neither logical nor easy to understand. I'll explain it to you –her mother said –. You're a good person, aren't you?

–Yes –Sophie replied shyly.

–Well, I agree with you, Sophie. I can say you're a good person –her mother said facing her daughter's sigh–. But daughter, we're all good people one way or another, and we're all bad people at some point, too, don't you think? Do you remember the world is neither black nor white, but gray?

—Yes, Mom, no one can be good forever and with everyone.

—That's right. So if someone thinks they have to be always a good person and don't see they also have a bad part, everytime they see a bad person they will criticize them in their mind, because they can't accept evil in his being. I don't know if I can explain myself.

—I think I understand —Sophie said, and asked—. What if I accept that I am good and bad at the same time?

–That's the key –her mother said–. If you accept the shadow, it disappears. On the contrary, the more radical you are denying your shadow, the more power you give it in your life, up to the level of not bearing the world, because you consider it an unpleasant place to live.

–Can I explain a secret to you, Sophie? –her mother asked with some mystery.

–Yes, of course –Sophie replied.

–I will tell you that many times happens that when a person has a child, the child himself ends up becoming the shadow of his parents. Can you believe it?

–Why is that happening? I don't get it –Sophie said.

—Well, parenting is a stressful thing, it's not easy, and dealing with clumsy, messy, squeaky, fickle little people... it's a big challenge; what happens then is that we get mad at those annoying little people, and instead of thinking that we have that part too, we end up projecting that this happens because the kids are just as annoying. As Jung said: *«Thinking is difficult, that is why most people judge».*

The mother breathed a sigh and went on to say:

—The easy way is to think that are the others who have to change for us to be happy —her mother finally said.

—Mom, am I your shadow? —Sophie asked in a concerned tone.

—Well, daughter —her mother said—, sometimes I felt it that way, but little by little I went learning and accepting that sometimes a son can be annoying, and that doesn't mean you stop loving him. Being a mother is a great learning, pretending to be «a good mother» can create a great shadow for you. It must be accepted that in the process of educating a child we will surely make many mistakes, and as always, we will learn from our mistakes.

And he gave her a big hug.

«What you deny subdues you,
what you accept transforms you»
Carl Gustav Jung

That night Sophie thought of the shadow, she said to herself that she had once felt that her mother did not accept her as she was, which for a moment filled her with sorrow because her greatest wish was that her mother was proud of her.

Sophie felt more calmed knowing the secret her mother had revealed to her, because now she knew she shouldn't be afraid of not being loved or accepted by her. It was her mother's issue, not hers. She understood her mother had fears and shadows, and although she had never considered it before, she realized her mother had also been little and had to learn everything she was now teaching to her. These thoughts caused her a deep sigh. She turned around in her bed and hugged the pillow before falling asleep.

9
BELIEFS

That afternoon Sophie sat down to do her homework in the kitchen. Her mother watched her sitting at the same table as her with her laptop open. She saw the girl looked nervous, kept blowing and crossing out what she was doing. Something had upset her.

—What's the matter with you, Sophie? —her mother asked finally after looking at her for a while.

—There will be a contest about reading aloud at school, and we can join in voluntarily.

—How interesting! —her mother exclaimed— I suppose you're going to take part, aren't you?

—I don't think so, I don't read aloud properly, I don't like to speak in public, I get nervous.

Her mother looked at her for a moment a little surprised to hear that claim; she had always considered her daughter very confident of her abilities.

—Do you think so, daughter? Why do you think you don't read well out loud? —her mother asked intriguedly.

—I don't know —replied Sophie.

—Maybe you should investigate where that belief comes from —her mother said—, because as Socrates said...

—Yes, yes, «know yourself» —Sophie said resigned.

—What we believe is more important than you think —her mother said—. People have a number of beliefs, some can be empowering, that is, they tell you that you are able to do something, and, on the contrary, there are others that are limiting and make you think that you can't do something, as it is the case of the reading contest.

—The truth is, I don't know why I have that belief —Sophie said—. I hadn't thought about it.

—Do you know the worst and the best about beliefs? —her mother said. That they come true, that is, if you think you don't know how to do something, like read well out loud, then you don't take parti in the contest and, in this way, for sure you don't win and you still think you don't read well out loud. I'll show you with a drawing.

Her mother stood up for a moment from her chair and went to look for paper and a pencil and started drawing a light bulb...

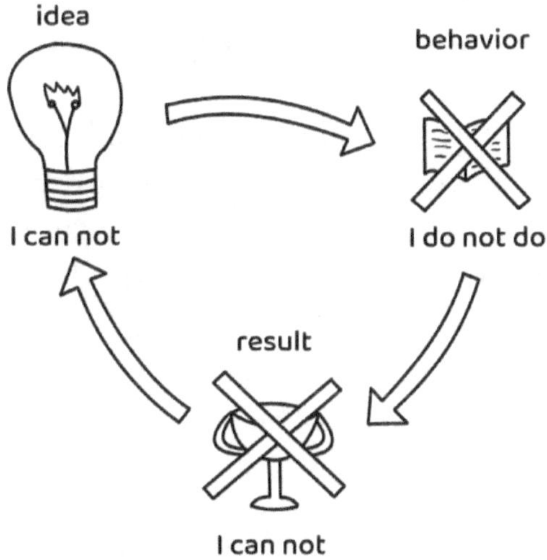

–If I think I can't, I don't do it and I finally can't do it –her mother said–. It's a circle that feeds back. In psychology this is called the SELF-FULFILLING PROPHECY, that is, we make what we think come true through our behavior.

–What can I do to know where my beliefs come from? –Sophie asked–. I really want to know myself, know if I'm good at reading aloud or not.

–Daughter, to know if you read well aloud, you only have to take part in the contest. You will see how you and your classmates read, and either you win or lose, you will know how you read. I want to explain a story to you. This is a history of Greek mythology.

Sophie wondered why her mother always explained stories of Greece to her, but she did not want to interrupt her and kept that question for another moment.

—Says the myth that a sculptor called Pygmalion made a sculpture of a very beautiful woman and liked her so much that he fell in love with her. He named her Galatea, and he would talk to her and take care of her as if she were a real woman. Then the goddess Aphrodite, seeing Pygmalion's love for the statue, brought the statue to life.

—You'll wonder why I'm explaining this story to you —her mother said—. You see, when some people have beliefs about each other, this generates something called the Pygmalion Effect; that is, if a person treats you in a certain way, in a way it influences you, it can happen that what they think about you will finally come true. As in the myth of Pygmalion, she treats the sculpture as if she was a real woman and eventually becomes a woman. I don't know if I can explain myself.

—It's a little confusing.

—You see —her mother said—, somehow people are influenced by what we are expected to be. Thus are formed beliefs about yourself, which are then fulfilled, as we have seen.

—Oh, I don't like that at all —Sophie said.

–Well, he thinks this effect can be both positive and negative –her mother said–. If you know it, you can make extraordinary things happen. As the great writer Goethe said: *«Treat a man as he is and he will remain as he is. Treat a man as he can become and should be and he will become what he can or should be».*

–This looks like the magic zone, where you can get extraordinary things, isn't it, Mom? –Sophie asked.

–It's pretty similar –her mother said–, but keep in mind that beliefs are before the action, in the light bulb. Do you remember the drawing? The first step is to believe that you can before you act.

–Yes, I remember –Sophie nodded.

–However, the magic zone belongs to the action. Beliefs are the foundation that forms SELF–ESTEEM; do you know what that is?

–A lot of times I've heard the word self-esteem, I guess it means loving yourself: self + esteem – Sophie replied.

–Well, self-esteem is a more complex concept than what it seems –her mother replied–. The word «esteem» actually comes from estimating, giving value to something, putting a price, that is, that you value yourself.

–So, can you value yourself well or badly? What does it depend on? –Sophie asked.

—Normally we talk about high or low self-esteem to say whether we value ourselves right or wrong as you say, but we can actually value ourselves in different ways. Five types of self-esteem are often described. Do you want to know them? —she asked.

—Yes! —Sophie replied.

—The five types of self-esteem are:

- **Stable highself-esteem:** self-confident person who does not allow himself to be influenced by the opinion of others.

- **Unstable highself-esteem:** person with high self-esteem, but who does not accept criticism. They let themselves be influenced by the opinion of others, do not accept failure and react with superiority when threatened.

- **Stable low self-esteem**: people who relies very little on their abilities, they are pessimistic and negative.

- **Unstable low self-esteem**: person who is estimated with little value, but when they are successful, they tend to increase their rating, that is, depending on the situation they can improve.

- **Inflated self-esteem:** it is the well-known false self-esteem, these are people who seem to have a high self-esteem because they are safe and arrogant, but they are people who seek recognition of others, their behavior actually hides a low self-esteem.

Sophie listened attentively to the explanation of the five types of self-esteem.

—As you'll see, it's important to have stable self-esteem —her mother said—, that it doesn't depend on other people's assessments and resists the Pygmalion effect. It's important that the first person who believes in you is yourself.

Sophie was thoughtful for a while and then said:

—If I believe in myself and treat myself as if I was very good at reading aloud, I could have a Pygmalion effect on myself and therefore read well —she said attentively to her mother's reaction.

—I see you've understood it perfectly —her mother said, nodding and with a big smile on her face. Sometimes things aren't that simple, though.

And she stirred her daughter's hair affectionately.

Sophie felt as if she had a super power, and she could do everything she set out to do. She thought that knowing how people's minds work can give many advantages in life, as well as being aware of one's own thoughts and observing how they influence our behavior.

The next day, Sophie signed up for the reading aloud competition. In the first week, different tests were performed and participants began to be eliminated. Sophie was preparing the text consciously: she kept practicing all day, taking advantage of any moment to rehearse details of pronunciation or rhythm. The reading belonged to a book about a child who had a somewhat peculiar family, in which descriptions and dialogues appeared. The difficult thing was to give a good intonation to some of the phrases; in addition, there were some words that required good vocalization, such as Egyptologist, kaleidoscope or transgressor, among others. They eventually elected a representative from each class. At her own surprise, Sophie won a place for the final.

This was held in the school's pavilion in front of all students. Sophie was very nervous as the contest had created a great expectation. When they headed to the great hall, her classmates encouraged her and shouted her name, and felt Sophie was her representative, as everybody wanted victory for her class.

Once in the pavilion, the contest was very close and, although Sophie was not the winner, she did so well that teachers and students praised her great speech, as she had toned each of the sentences clearly and greatly, making use of her theatrical skills successfully. Sophie was very satisfied and felt that she had learned a lot from this experience. She said to herself that she would never again reject the opportunity to participate in something, just because of the thought that she would not do well, and that it was always worth a try.

«Your values are not defined by your words,
but by your actions«
Anonymous

10
VALUES

That day the whole family went to eat at a restaurant. While they were waiting for the waiter to come, they spoke animatedly and explained to Sophie's father and brother what the girl had learned in the last days.

Sophie had begun to observe her beliefs, and when she thought about whether or not she could do something, she wondered why. That had made her realize that in many occasions she did not know why she had certain ideas, and in this way she was getting used not to give anything for sure, and questioning whether there was any reason to think that way.

–Mom, I think I have it already clear –Sophie said–. If I believe in myself, I have a self-esteem that is good and stable and I am also brave, I can go for what I want, right? –she asked.

–Totally true –her mother said–, however, do you know what you want and what you want it for?

–Well, –Sophie replied, hesitantly–. What I want is what makes me vibrate.

–Yes, but I haven't asked you why you want it but what you want it for –her mother said.

–Isn't that the same thing?

–Not at all, the question «why» and «what for» give very different answers, –her mother clarified –. When you ask «WHY» the answer isn't usually very interesting, it's a question that tells you things you already know, it's like saying nothing. On the other hand, when you ask «WHAT FOR» you have to think in the depths inside you, and that's when your VALUES appear. The answers we give to the «what for» are located in the submerged part of the iceberg; do you remember how that part is called?

She looked at her daughter waiting for her answer.

–The unconscious –Sophie replied–. But I don't understand, I don't see the difference between the two questions, they look the same to me.

–I'll give you an example, but first let's order the food.

At that moment the waiter arrived and everyone said what they wanted to eat, Sophie ordered a burger and potatoes and a bottle of water. When the waiter left with everyone's orders, the conversation continued.

–For example –her mother continued to speak–, you've ordered a burger with potatoes and water to drink. Why did you choose that?

–Because I always ask for that, I like it.
–Well, why do you like it?
–Because it's delicious, it tastes good.

–And why is it delicious?

–Because it carries ingredients that I like.

–And why does it carry ingredients that you like? –Her mother asked, adding: –We could be asking questions for hours, and we wouldn't get to anything concrete; conversely, each answer generates many other questions. And the same would happen with many other different topics: the origin of meat, why living beings feed, why we like tasty food, if it has additives... Now, Sophie, –what did you order a burger and potatoes for?

–Hmmm, for...

After thinking for a while she said:

–To feed me, –she replied at last.

–Well, what do you want to feed yourself for?

–To be strong and healthy.

–Do you realize that we have come to a value, that it is health, and that there you can no longer ask? –Sophie's mother concluded–. It's very different to think you eat something because it's delicious than to think you eat something to be healthy. When you think about values you connect with who you are and what motivates you to do things. It's important to know your values.

Sophie reflected for a moment while she was eating chips with her hands. Her brother looked at her attentively to her reaction, the conversation had created expectation in the family and everyone had observed questions and answers between mother and daughter as a tennis match.

—How many values do people have? —Sophie asked finally.

—That depends on each person —her mother replied—, but it seems interesting that we know our values so that we know what guides us in our lives, don't you think?

—Yes, but how can we know them?

—If you want to know your values we will have to do an exercise. Are you interested? When we get home, I'll explained it to you —her mother suggested.

—Sure, I like doing your exercises —Sophie said.

When they got home Sophie's mother searched through her notebooks and pulled out a sheet where there was a grid with a few boxes to fill in:

Area	Value	CURRENT STATE	DESIRED STATE
House			
Personal care			
Studies			
Family			
Money management			
Leisure			
Friends			
Vocation			
...			

–What are the areas? –Sophie asked.

–These are the significant issues of your life. Depending on the stage of life we are in, they may change. For example: at your age there is an important part that are the studies, but there is no portion for motherhood. Do you understand?

Sophie nodded.

–Before you start filling out the table you should check if these are your areas at present. There's space to include more and you can remove some if necessary.

Sophie nodded.

–The next thing is to find out the value behind each of them.

–How do I know what value there is? –Sophie asked.

–Through the question «for what reason» –said her mother–. Just like we did at the restaurant. For example: for the «HOUSE» area, you have to ask the following question: Why do I want to live in your house? And in the «FRIENDS» area, for what reason do I have friends?... Like this with each of the areas.

Sophie went to her room with the sheet in her hand. She looked at the areas for a while and removed some that she replaced with other ones. She then asked the question «for what reason» in each of them and realized something that surprised her. Values were repeated, she thought people had as many values as areas of life, but she was wrong: three values came out in total.

When she was done, she went downstairs to the living room looking for her mother, who was sitting on the couch reading a book.

–I've got it –she said.

—Well, now we're going to assess how that area is right now and how you wish it were —said her mother—. If you doubt, think about the time you spend on it, that can help you value it.

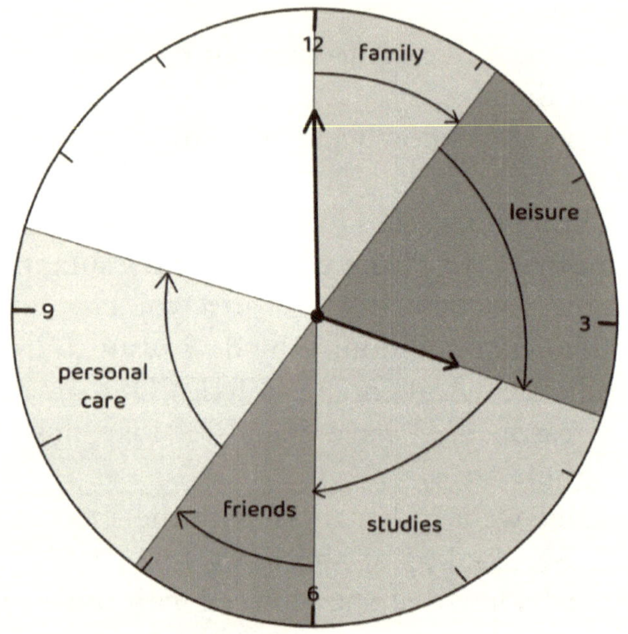

—If I spend time in an area, does that mean it's important for me?

—That's right —her mother said—. Life is a matter of priorities. We can't have it all. When you spend time in one area you have to take it away from another, because time is limited. There is where you're going to have to choose what you spend your time on and, most importantly, why you want to dedicate it to that area.

—I don't know if I'm getting it right, Mom —said Sophie finally afterwards, looking at the board for a long time—. What should guide my life is what makes me vibrate, but in each of the areas of my life there are values that are also a guide, right?

—That's right, daughter —replied her mother—, we need the values because, if you look at them they are related to our needs. We sometimes seek safety in the family for example, fun in leisure, self-realization at work... Gradually we will build our puzzle piece by piece.

—But what is what guides me? What makes me vibrate, what I want to have, my values? —asked Sophie.

—They're all guides in your life —said her mother—. We are made up of a number of things that are forces that pull you. As if you were a puppet with invisible threads, which at certain times make you act in a certain way. Maybe it's time to put some names in the iceberg. Here's how you'll see it much clearer:

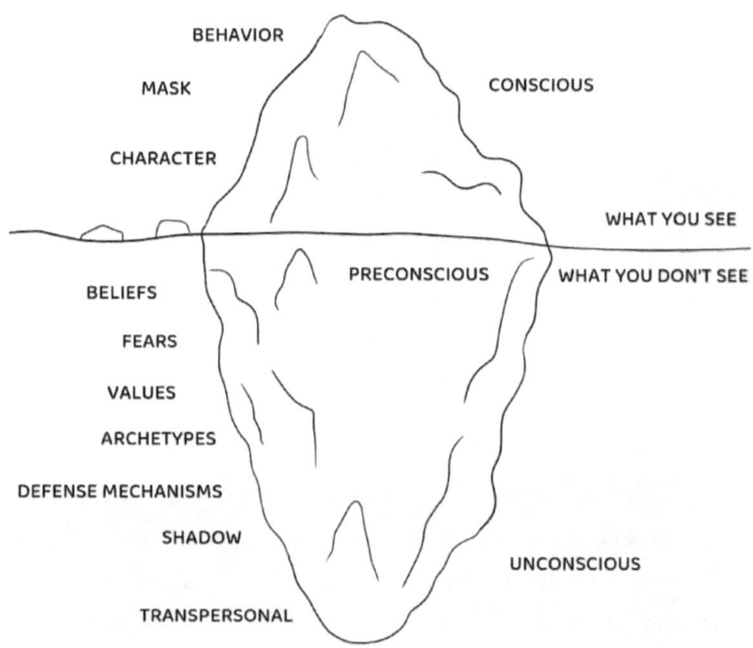

«When I let go of what I am,
I become what I might be«
LAO–TSÉ

11
TRANSPERSONAL

Sophie looked at the iceberg for a long time, gradually integrating everything she had learned, and observed that people's visible part is a very small portion: their actions, their behavior, their mask, in short, the character with its various roles.

Instead, almost everything she had discovered in chats with her mother belonged to the submerged world she was unaware of. Now she realized that she hadn't been able to see it before because they were hidden, she didn't even know they existed.

In the hidden there were: fears, beliefs she did not know where they came from, values for the different areas of her life, a main archetype that guided her in secret, as well as her shadow or defense mechanisms. A whole series of things that could be better or worse, but she needed to know if she wanted to be the owner of her own life.

She read each of the words until she reached the depths of the iceberg, where the word «transpersonal» was written.

—Mom —Sophie said—. There's a word I don't understand in the iceberg. At the bottom, it says «transpersonal». What does it mean? —she asked.

—Right, there's something I haven't explained to you yet —said her mother—. Transpersonal means that it goes beyond the personal, it refers to aspects that transcend the person, that go further from knowing yourself, I don't know if I'm making myself clear.

–What does it mean aspects that transcend? – asked Sophie.

–To transcend means going further, to an unknown area –replied her mother–. It is a development of consciousness that surpasses who you are as an individual, beyond the body and mind.

–Like the magic zone? –asked Sophie.

–Let's see –said her mother, watching Sophie's puzzled face–. I'll explain it another way.

Her mother got up and went to heat water to prepare an infusion. It was time to talk about the «Myth of the Cave».

–Sophie, I have to explain to you another story, it is Plato's «Myth of the Cave», which was a disciple of Socrates. Maybe you know him.

–No, I don't know him– Sophie replied.

–It is a book which explains a situation of a group of people who are chained to a wall in a cave, and have been there their whole lives. Behind these people there is a wall and a fire, and this casts shadows on the wall. And behind this wall there are other people who have objects, animals... and raise them precisely to show their shadows. In this way, chained people have names for those shadows, because that's their reality.

–Poor people, chained for life, what a sad story –Sophie said.

—That's right, daughter, but in the myth it happens that a slave manages to escape from his chains and is able to see what's behind the wall, and discovers that he had never seen reality, but his cast shadow. Then, he warns that he must look away from the fire because, as he had never looked directly at the light before, it damages his eyes, and in this situation he prefers to continue looking into the darkness, which he is used to.

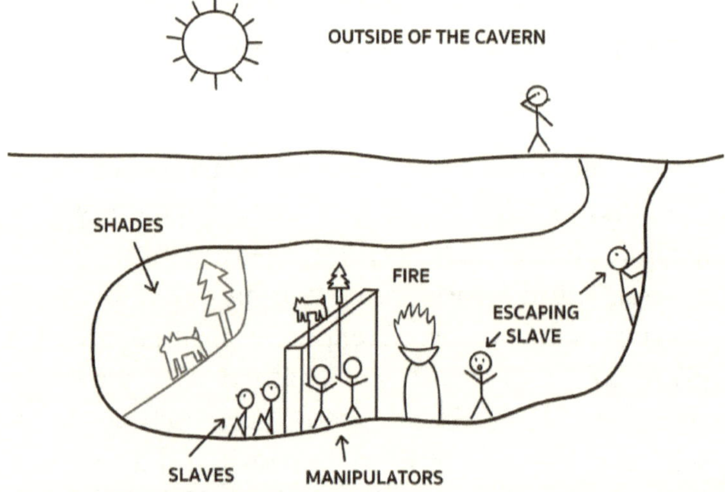

—It would be normal if you've never seen the light —Sophie said.

—Now imagine that person caming out of the cave and looking at the sunlight. He'd still be more upset, his eyes would hurt, and he wouldn't like to leave the cave.

Sophie was trying to imagine the situation, she thought that it had already happened to her: when she was in a dark room and went outside, in the sunlight, for a while, she could see nothing. Her mother went on to explain:

—Plato uses this myth to explain that human beings are like those chained people who do not see the truth, but a superficial reality. When Plato speaks about the released person, he refers to the awakening of that lie through discovery, learning, wondering about our beliefs, getting to know each other better.

—And what does it mean when they leave the cave? —Sophie asked.

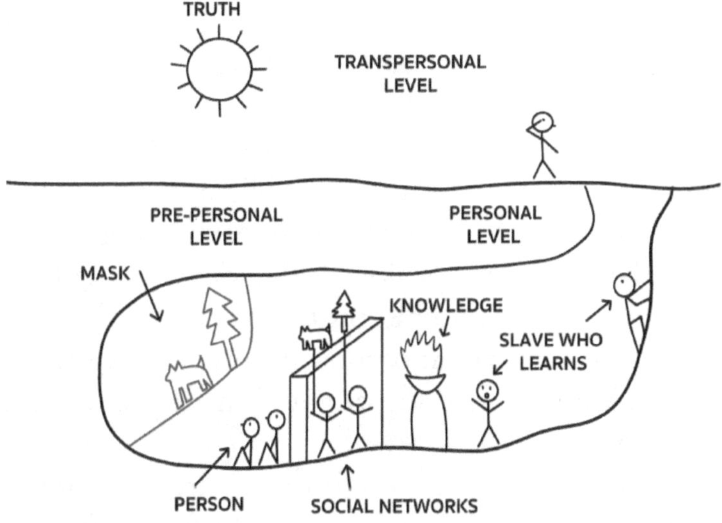

—To leave the cave is to reach the transpersonal. If the cast shadows are our character, our mask, the cave is our consciousness where we know our essence, our needs, our values... So the outside of the cave is what's beyond our iceberg, it represents the open sea.

–What happens in the myth when the person leaves the cave? –asked Sophie.

–In the myth, when the person knows the truth of the outside, he returns to the cave to explain it to his trapped companions, but they do not understand it, mock the person and treat the person as he was mad. However, Plato, like his master Socrates, believed it was an obligation to share the truth and spread knowledge.

–I agree –she said–, because maybe not everyone has the strength to free themselves from chains, and that's what teachers are for.

Sophie's mother looked for a while at her daughter; she could almost perceive how she was awaking, how new paths full of light were opened in her mind to be explored with each dialogue.

–Plato's myth speaks of the development of consciousness –said her mother.

–I don't understand consciousness developing, or you know something or you don't know it. Isn't that right?

–People since we were born we are developing –her mother explained–, we go through different stages of learning, because we have to learn everything practically from scratch. Human beings are one of the living beings which born knowing less, but that is precisely why he has a greater ability to learn. In this way, we gradually go through different stages and develop. In this development there is learning in almost every aspect of life: at motor level, mental, emotional, moral... All of these levels have stages of development well defined.

Sophie nodded.

–Good. There is also the development of consciousness, that is, about the knowledge of one's own thought. There is a philosopher and writer named Ken Wilber who describes three stages:

- **Pre-personal level**: before being aware of being a person, the person has not yet been aware of their own mind, nor they have formed their personality.

- **Personal level**: the person is aware of being a differentiated individual; it is the conventional level, that is, the most normal.

- **Transpersonal level**: the person becomes aware of belonging to something greater, acquires social, ecological and spiritual awareness.

–How do I know if I have a transpersonal consciousness? –asked Sophie.

–I have summarized to you the three levels of the consciousness development –her mother said–, but each level has three more stages that need to be overcome, it is a long path that you will gradually go through. There are things you'll assimilate easier and things that are going to confuse you at first, but do not ever be in a hurry. Remember that you have to get used to the light to be able to see clearly.

Sophie nodded.

–Daughter, if I ask you who you are, what would you answer?

Sophie reflected for a moment and answered:

–I would say it's me with my character, with my beliefs, my fears, my values, my defense mechanisms, my dominant archetype, my shadow... I don't know if I'm forgetting something.

–Well, daughter –finally said her mother–. Although we still have many things to learn and that personality can be seen from many different fields, Now, I can see you know a little bit more about the world around you and yourself.

That week Sophie had learned many concepts that she didn't know so far. The most important thing was not what she had learned, but she knew there was much more to learn. That encouraged her to such an extent that she was determined to take her library license to go and look for all those unread books she had on her list. Now, her dilemma was which one to start with.

Sophie was a little more aware of is the new meaning of freedom; she realized there were many hidden forces guiding her and that the way to be free from those threads or chains was through knowledge. She knew the learning path was long and hard, but it was full of exciting things she couldn't even imagine, and she was thrilled about it.

Sophie felt like she was the owner of the hidden forces behind the visible. She felt like a horsewoman riding a horse she could guide on its way through an extensive meadow.

THE END

WHO AM I?

Annex
TEST ON THE TWELVE ARCHETYPES

Mark with a cross, with which of the following statements you really feel identified with. Keep in mind that the statement should represent you, it's not about occasional situations, but they must define you:

Statement	N°
1. When it's the end of the school and we go outside I think we have to be careful just in case any unforeseen events arise	8
2. When we do a group work it is usually me who distributes the tasks	6
3. In class I usually help struggling classmates	4
4. They usually choose me when it's time to speak in public	10
5. If I'm chosen to do something I don't feel like doing, I say it and I don't do so	11
6. I'm often told I'm funny	2

7. I really like hiking especially because it's like an adventure	5
8. What I like to play the most is to imagine stories	3
9. At school, it sometimes bothers me that there is too much noise	12
10. I like to play battles at recess	7
11. When someone forgets breakfast I think they are a disaster, they are always the same ones who leave it all	6
12. My friends often say that I like to swim against the tide	11
13. I am messy at home	11
14. I still have my favorite cuddly toy kept	1
15. I usually speak in a high but calm tone	9
16. When I speak I usually draw everyone's attention	10
17. In the cinema I especially like movies where there are disputes	7

18. My parents often tell me that I am very responsible	6
19. Others come to me when they need to be defended	7
20. When someone wants to know something, they usually ask me	12
21. I'm rather a restless person	11
22. I like to be cautious and be careful, you never know what can happen	8
23. Sometimes I suffer because I am afraid of new situations	8
24. I usually convince others of what I want	10
25. I am really concerned that people suffer for me	4
26. Sometimes I feel like I need to know more about one topic and I research it	12
27. I am an artistic person, I like creating new things	3
28. I enjoy being kind to others	9

29. When I study for an exam, I review it many times to make sure I will do it right	6
30. I like to tell jokes	2
31. Sometimes people disappoint me, I expected them to take me into account	8
32. I like to do quiet activities where I can enjoy a good landscape	9
33. I'm not usually afraid, they tell me I'm daring	5
34. I am a competitive person, I really like to win	7
35. I am a very observant person, I realize small details	12
36. I can't stand to see someone suffer, I have to help them	4
37. I am a very affectionate person, I like to embrace others	1
38. I like hint and discovering treasures games	5
39. When there is a fight I worry about bringing peace	9

40. I find it hard to get to the places on time, I am usually late	3
41. I don't mind sacrificing myself if I can help someone	4
42. I'm a romantic person	1
43. My parents say I don't listen to what they tell me	11
44. Sometimes I have not said the whole truth to get what I want	10
45. My favorite subject is art	3
46. If I run my team I'm sure we will win	6
47. I think it is important for each person to do what they want and what make them happy	9
48. I can't stand boredom	2
49. Sometimes I think that if we all protest together we can make something change	11
50. One of the things I love most is traveling	5

51. Sometimes I know what people think, I have a lot of intuition	10
52. My best friend is forever	1
53. I consider myself a strong person, I can achieve what I propose	7
54. I'm sometimes alone to be able to concentrate better	12
55. I don't mind sharing out my food if someone is hungrier than me	4
56. When there's a fight I'll see if I can help solving it	8
57. I usually check the suitcase when I go on a trip to make sure I do not forget anything	6
58. Sometimes my parents scold me because they say I'm shameless	5
59. I like drawing with many colored pencils at home	3
60. If I find a wounded animal, I can't avoid picking it up to heal it	4

61. I have the ability to bring together a group of people to do something	6
62. Sometimes others don't take me into account	8
63. Sometimes I enjoy being alone doing something creative	3
64. I like doing things in my way without following the rules strictly	11
65. I have no difficulty in fighting for what I want	7
66. I am passionate about setting up a surprise party and surprising someone I love	1
67. When I hear a word I don't normally know, I look for it in the dictionary	12
68. Even if I don't know where a road leads, I like going and finding out	5
69. I usually have fun and laugh a lot	2
70. I immediately realize when someone is not well	4

71. By intuition I usually know why some people act in a certain way	10
72. I do not like conflict, I enjoy being friendly with everybody.	9

TEST RESULT

Count the times each of the following numbers are marked:

1	2	3	4	5	6	7	8	9	10	11	12

Then mark the code that has come out a greater number of times. That's the archetype that has the most influence on you. You can see its features in the following summary:

ARCHETYPE 1 – THE LOVER

Description

You are a person driven to do what you love, you live your life with passion, whether towards a profession, an idea or a project.

You are a person who keeps in mind romantic and idealized love, you seek the balance between giving affection and receiving it. You enjoy the beauty of things and value through the senses cosmetic balance.

POSITIVE FEATURES – LIGHT

You are an affectionate, loving and passionate person.
You have a great enthusiasm for life. You try to do what you love.
You are a sociable person who makes bonds easily.
You tend to make people happy; you even care more about other's happiness than yours.

NEGATIVE FEATURES – SHADOW

You can become a jealous and possessive person.
Sometimes you can envy other's happiness.
An obsessive fixation may be given for the loved object or person.
It can give lack of emotional control, depression or anxiety.
There is a risk of losing one's identity to adapt to others and please them.

ARCHETYPE 2 – THE JESTER

Description

You are a joyful and vital person who wants others to enjoy and appreciate the joy of life. You focus on enjoying the present moment. You run away from boredom and that's why you seek to entertain with all kinds of actions.
You have an independent, creative and original thinking. You're not afraid of gettting out of the conventional, thus you're funny and original. You can use an exaggerated or absurd tone.

POSITIVE FEATURES – LIGHT

You make others feel good.
You're flexible and fun–loving.
You are a person with great creativity and innovation.
You have sense of humor.

NEGATIVE FEATURES – SHADOW

You can go over the line to be funny and sometimes you find it hard to see the limit.
You need constant stimulation and flattery.
You can become unstable to entertain others.
You can be rude and offensive.

ARCHETYPE 3 – THE CREATOR

Description

You have a deep yearning for freedom and you love the novel. You love experimenting and transforming things to bring up something whole new.

You're witty, nonconforming and self–sufficient. You have a lot of imagination, you're full of genius. Sometimes you can be fickle and you think more than what you do.

You represent creativity, the need of the human being to express.

POSITIVE FEATURES – LIGHT

You're a creative person who attracts you to novel features.
You need to express.
You have aesthetic sense.
You don't easily accept rules and limits.
You're an idealist, you're looking for a better world.
You're an impulsive person.

NEGATIVE FEATURES – SHADOW

You don't fit the schedules well. You're disorganized.
You may experience distress, anxiety, or melancholy.
You have attachment to the past.
You can be narcissistic.
You may have emotional instability.

ARCHETYPE 4 – THE CARER

Description

You are a person with great compassion and sacrificial capacity. You dedicate yourself to help others without hesitation. You are protector with others and have a lot of understanding and generosity.
You are a person with great control and stability.
You have a lot of sensitivity to the suffering of others.

POSITIVE FEATURES – LIGHT

You're a good, compassionate, empathetic person.
You stay calm and you're optimistic.
Always willing to help.
You fix your eyes on others, rather than on yourself.

NEGATIVE FEATURES – SHADOW

You can be an overbearing person.
You can abuse power.
Sometimes you can get too worried.

ARCHETYPE 5 – THE EXPLORER

Description

You seek adventure with freedom and independence. You're a daring traveler.
You have a free, bold, independent and somewhat sassy personality. You're not afraid of challenges. You're looking for a never found ideal.
You represent the search for your own identity.
You have trouble choosing the path you want to follow, you need help and guidance.

POSITIVE FEATURES – LIGHT

You enjoy freedom.
You're not afraid of challenges.
You are a person open to novelty and adventure.
You're an entrepreneur and a brave person.

NEGATIVE FEATURES – SHADOW

You're a restless person.
You can get shameless.
You take action when you don't have a defined route; you run the risk of getting lost along the way.
You're never satisfied, you always want more.

ARCHETYPE 6 – THE RULER

Description

You are a person with a great capacity for leadership, to direct and lead people.
As a leader you are the one who understands the needs of the group best and works for them. You can think about the collective before than self interests.
You have great sustenance, protection and guidance over those you care for.

POSITIVE FEATURES – LIGHT

You have conscious leadership skills.
You're responsible with you and with other people.
You have easiness in managing thriving businesses.
You take responsibility for successes and failures.
Ability to gather people.
Ability to adapt to life's difficulties.

NEGATIVE FEATURES – SHADOW

You can become an arrogant, aggressive, uncompromising person.
You're usually closed to unforeseen events.
You have a great need to control.
You suffer from a lack of trust in other people.
You can be selfish and tyrant.

ARCHETYPE 7 – THE HERO

Description

You are a person who when facing a problem feels an inner call to solve it. You're a fighter and you have the courage to deal with difficult situations.
You are a person who takes control of your own life. You throw yourself into the struggle for what you believe and you learn and grow as a person in that process.

POSITIVE FEATURES – LIGHT

You're a successful person in life.
You are a strong, firm, determined, dynamic and resilient person.
You have the power of fulfillment.

NEGATIVE FEATURES – SHADOW

You can become an aggressive, competitive and disloyal person.
You can be reckless.
You usually have a life full of conflicts.

ARCHETYPE 8 – THE ORPHAN

Description

You are a person who recognizes and avoids situations that can harm you. You are conservative and you're trying to protect yourself from feeling abandoned, hurt or victimized.
You are a defender of your well–being, sometimes denying the possibility of new experiences because of fear.

POSITIVE FEATURES – LIGHT

You have the capacity to overcome and recover from the disappointments of life.
You take care of yourself, you're self–sufficient.
You have a great capacity for empathy, helping others, and sharing feelings.
You are prudent, you prefer security, you are realistic and with a lot of common sense.

NEGATIVE FEATURES – SHADOW

You can get victimized.
You expect special treatment from others.
You take no responsibility.
You may have a feeling of abandonment, betrayal, and disappointment.
You have a cynical humor.

ARCHETYPE 9 – THE INNOCENT

Description

You live in simplicity and longing for happiness. You are characterized by being good, kind and confident.

You have an optimistic attitude and you defend the freedom to be yourself. You see the bright side of everything.

You enjoy when you feel adapted to the world. You like to please, belong and be recognized by others.

POSITIVE FEATURES – LIGHT

You like peace, simplicity and serenity.
You're optimistic, you have a positive vision.
You're looking for happiness.
You have a desire to please and belong to the group.
You fight for your freedom.

NEGATIVE FEATURES – SHADOW

You might become the victim.
You demand help from others.
You don't take responsibility for problems and difficulties.
You can be narcissistic.
You can become a capricious and chaotic person.

ARCHETYPE 10 – THE MAGICIAN

Description

You have an incredible power of communication. A great ability to communicate with other people and with nature.

You represent youth, the overture towards the possibilities of life.

You are a person with great ability to convince and influence others, doing the impossible through the word.

POSITIVE FEATURES – LIGHT

You have the power of communication, awareness and transformation of reality.

You have a connection with nature.

Great ability to work, open-minded and capacity for innovation.

You are an entrepreneurial person with great power of realization and trust.

NEGATIVE FEATURES – SHADOW

You may have a tendency to lie and manipulate.

You can be impulsive.

You can become selfish, evil, treacherous.

You can find yourself alone.

ARCHETYPE 11 – THE OUTLAW

Description

You're a person who sees the world in a new way. You have a need to challenge all limiting beliefs.
You are characterized by disobedience and peaceful resistance. Your rebellion is marked by being calm and altruistic.
This rebellion entails the renunciation of your personal interests in favor of a greater good.

POSITIVE FEATURES – LIGHT

You have the gift of patience.
You have the ability to see the world with a new perspective.
You have the capacity of sacrifice for a noble cause.
You respect people. You have great wisdom.
You don't use violence and you have self–control.
You make a peaceful critique of social conventions.

NEGATIVE FEATURES – SHADOW

You can get to aggressive rebellion.
Sometimes you want to impose your ideas.
You're a person who can be sufferer and resentful.
You may feel like you're not in the world.

ARCHETYPE 12 – THE WISE

Description

You are a person with great wisdom. You live in solitude and silence. Your goal is the search for truth, the search for how the world works.

You're in constant self–known process. You have serenity, patience and autonomy.

You're introspective, you'd rather reflect alone than be with other people.

POSITIVE FEATURES – LIGHT

You break the conventions and you seek your own truth.
You are a very curious, objective and eagle-eyed person.
You are balanced, you learn from mistakes.
You are very persistent.
You have knowledge and lucidity.

NEGATIVE FEATURES – SHADOW

You can tend to isolation.
You can suffer from depression and sadness.
You can become a cold and insensitive person.
You have a tendency to be perfectionist, intolerant and arrogant.

ABOUT THE AUTHOR

Rosa Domingo was born in Barcelona. She studied psychology at the University of Barcelona and her other passion was always drawing. After working for years in the field of Human Resources, she decided to study a master's degree in orientation of cognitive behavioral psychology and later a degree in psychopedagogenics. She uses her academic knowledge and clinical practice to spread psychology topics by bringing them closer to the general public through simple and easy-to-understand language.